THE COMPLETE IDIOT'S GUIDE TO

Raising Chickens

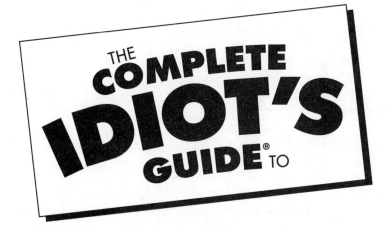

Raising Chickens

by Jerome D. Belanger

ALPHA

A member of Penguin Group (USA) Inc.

ALPHA BOOKS

Published by the Penguin Group

Penguin Group (USA) Inc., 375 Hudson Street, New York, New York 10014, USA

Penguin Group (Canada), 90 Eglinton Avenue East, Suite 700, Toronto, Ontario M4P 2Y3, Canada (a division of Pearson Penguin Canada Inc.)

Penguin Books Ltd., 80 Strand, London WC2R 0RL, England

Penguin Ireland, 25 St. Stephen's Green, Dublin 2, Ireland (a division of Penguin Books Ltd.)

Penguin Group (Australia), 250 Camberwell Road, Camberwell, Victoria 3124, Australia (a division of Pearson Australia Group Pty. Ltd.)

Penguin Books India Pvt. Ltd., 11 Community Centre, Panchsheel Park, New Delhi—110 017, India

Penguin Group (NZ), 67 Apollo Drive, Rosedale, North Shore, Auckland 1311, New Zealand (a division of Pearson New Zealand Ltd.)

Penguin Books (South Africa) (Pty.) Ltd., 24 Sturdee Avenue, Rosebank, Johannesburg 2196, South Africa

Penguin Books Ltd., Registered Offices: 80 Strand, London WC2R 0RL, England

International Standard Book Number: 978-1-59257-986-0
Library of Congress Catalog Card Number: 2009937012

12 11 10   8 7 6 5 4 3 2 1

Interpretation of the printing code: The rightmost number of the first series of numbers is the year of the book's printing; the rightmost number of the second series of numbers is the number of the book's printing. For example, a printing code of 10-1 shows that the first printing occurred in 2010.

Printed in the United States of America

Publisher: *Marie Butler-Knight*
Editorial Director: *Mike Sanders*
Senior Managing Editor: *Billy Fields*
Acquisitions Editor: *Tom Stevens*
Development Editor: *Michael Thomas*
Production Editor: *Kayla Dugger*

Copy Editor: *Kelly D. Henthorne*
Cover Designer: *Bill Thomas*
Book Designer: *Trina Wurst*
Indexer: *Heather McNeill*
Layout: *Becky Batchelor*
Proofreader: *John Etchison*

Contents at a Glance

Contents

Introduction

Many animal fads have come and gone: Belgian hares, ostriches, chinchillas, and 150 years ago, even chickens. In most cases interest rose quickly, and so did prices, as demand exceeded supply. Some people paid more than $50 in the 1850s bubble—more than $1,200 in today's money—for one chicken!

The current interest in chickens is different. Only time will tell whether it's a lasting interest, but it's not a fad. It certainly isn't based on any illusions about getting rich, and prices haven't ballooned. In fact, much of it is just the opposite: a desire for a simpler life, closer to nature, closer contact with our food, and better food, even if it does cost a little more.

According to a reporter writing in the *Hartford Advocate* in March 2009, there are two groups of urban chicken farmers—the low-income, mostly immigrant group that keeps chickens as a side business by selling extra meat and eggs; and upper-class environmentalists who keep boutique hens as pets, but eat or share the eggs with friends. Maybe things are different in Hartford, but I can assure you that in most of the rest of the country, there are thousands of backyard chickens between those two extremes. In other words, there truly is a chicken for everybody.

The personal agrisystem of feeding food scraps to chickens which then produce eggs for breakfast and fertilizer for the tomatoes has great personal appeal. People like the idea that they take care of the chickens, and the chickens take care of them, in a cause-and-effect relationship seldom seen so clearly in today's world. Food is *not* manufactured in the back room of the A&P, or today's equivalent.

Although that relationship transforms the chicken from a mere commodity to a somewhat more important and integral part of life, it doesn't go nearly far enough. Because once we understand how our relationship with *Gallus gallus* has changed since the beginning, and how that change has affected both of us, we get a new view not only of the chicken, but of ourselves.

If that sounds overblown or a bit much to lay on the simple chicken, please humor me for at least a few pages. See if I can convince you that a chicken is much more fascinating than you ever imagined.

Yes, chickens are a commodity today, the way we treat them. We'll talk about the four reasons for raising chickens, including the commodity, or profit factor. But chickens are not all the same, as we'll see when we discuss their family tree. Presumably, you want to raise a few of these birds for one or more of the four reasons, and I'll provide some advice on doing that, including housing, feeding, and health. And if these topics make you wonder about organic eggs, free-range eggs, and antibiotics in feeds, you have come to the right place for some answers.

Mingled in with these "practical" matters are others that, I hope, will prevent you from ever again thinking of a chicken as just a piece of meat. Did you know, for example, that chickens "breathe" through some of their bones? Why eggshells come in different colors, or for that matter, how an egg is layed? How much do you know about chicken behavior, or their language? (Of course they have a language!)

Think of chicken appreciation like going through an art gallery. Someone who knows absolutely nothing about art might look at all the pretty pictures (and some that aren't) and decide which ones they like, if any. They'll leave a little bit richer for the experience, but not much.

On the other hand, a knowledgeable observer might know something about the artists, and the nuances of style, periods, and techniques. That person will enjoy the exhibit far more than the unenlightened one and will gain vastly more from it.

It's the same with chickens. The more you know about them, the more you'll appreciate them. My hope and intention is that this book will be a basic course in chicken appreciation—and that you'll appreciate them so much, you'll want a few of your own to enjoy, close-up.

Extras

Even covering all these "extraneous" topics (to the person who is only interested in white meat, dark meat, and eggs, that is) doesn't allow me to cover the *whole* chicken. So I've added little tidbits to peck at as we go along.

Cacklings

Tips that might save you time, money, or effort will be found in boxes like this one.

def•i•ni•tion

These sidebars define unfamiliar terms or terms with unique meanings in the world of chickens.

Fox Alert

On rare occasions there might be situations or conditions that could be hazardous to you or your birds. I'll alert you to those with a word of warning.

Cocktail Conversation

Whether you use these snippets of miscellaneous information at a cocktail party, the water cooler, or maybe even in a tweet is up to you, but they will set you apart as someone who knows a thing or two about chickens.

Acknowledgments

Many people have participated in the making of this book, most of them associated in some way with *Backyard Poultry* magazine. Editor Elaine Belanger was very helpful with advice and ideas, and editorial assistant Samantha Ingersoll went well beyond the call of duty to help with the photos. Most of the wonderful pictures themselves came from the magazine's readers, who graciously allowed me to share them with you in this book. Other readers contributed comments and questions that provide a much broader view of the poultry world than I would otherwise command, based only on my own experience.

And then there's Diane, who once again had to put up with a "retired" husband who was unavailable during the heart of the busy gardening season. Now that I'm retiring for the third time, maybe I'm finally home to roost for good.

Special Thanks to the Technical Reviewer

The Complete Idiot's Guide to Raising Chickens was reviewed by an expert who double-checked the accuracy of what you'll learn here, to help us ensure that this book gives you everything you need to know about raising chickens. Special thanks are extended to Mike Banks.

Mike Banks is a proud husband, father, and grandfather, and is currently a graduate student at Purdue University in West Lafayette, Indiana. His research includes multiple poultry species with emphasis on amino acid nutrition, energy efficiency, and mineral utilization of co-products from the ethanol industry.

Trademarks

1

Chickens for All!

In This Chapter

- ◆ Chickens can be self-sufficient
- ◆ A chicken for every purpose
- ◆ Some legal and economic aspects
- ◆ How to get started raising chickens

There are about 24 billion chickens in the world. That's more than 3½ chickens for every human on Earth.

Shouldn't at least a few of them be in *your* backyard?

Raising Chickens Is Simple

Your great-grandparents probably raised chickens, and they did it without reading any books. Not very long ago, almost every farm had a few chickens, and poultry-keeping wasn't unusual in towns, either.

But then, there wasn't a whole lot to know. A hen layed eggs and sat on them until they hatched. After the 21-day incubation period, she reappeared in the barnyard, followed by a lively clutch of fluffy, peeping chicks. The chicks grew up, and the process continued. Simple.

It's a little more complicated today, but mostly because humans make it so. If you've been to places like Key West, Florida, or the Hawaiian Island of Kauai, you've seen feral chickens that take care of themselves, even among humans who try to discourage them! In colder climates they do need food and shelter during the winter, but that doesn't have to be complicated either.

Chickens run wild in many places in the world, even in cities: on the streets, in grocery store parking lots, and sometimes in front of restaurants where a certain colonel is known for chicken of a different kind. Here are some feral chickens in downtown Panama City, Panama.

(Photo: David Chase, Seymour, Missouri)

So what do you really and truly, absolutely have to know to begin raising chickens? Not much. And that's how many people start out.

On the other hand, we could talk about chickens all day and half the night, and many people do that, too. Chickens are fascinating creatures in many ways, and we'll touch on a few interesting facts about them that aren't essential to know but that make wonderful cocktail conversation. But right now you probably have some more basic questions, such as: What's really involved? Is chicken-raising right for me? How do I get started?

Why Chickens?

There are several reasons to raise chickens. The main one, covering the vast majority of those 24 billion birds, is to make money. An urban backyarder with 3 or 4 hens, or even a small farmer with 50 to 100, obviously isn't going to make any money worth crowing about, so I trust money isn't one of your reasons.

Another reason is to provide eggs and meat. Although small flocks can provide more than enough eggs for a family, all of those backyard chickens combined (probably several hundred thousand worldwide, although no one knows for certain) don't produce as many eggs as one modern "egg factory."

> **Cocktail Conversation**
>
> Sixty egg-producing companies have more than one million layers each; twelve have more than five million each. Keep these numbers in mind as we discuss the importance of small, backyard flocks.

For the majority of urban backyard poultry keepers, meat doesn't even enter the picture. Butchering is seldom permitted in cities and suburbs. Backyard chickens might lay the most wonderful eggs in the world, but even though it might start out as a good excuse, raising chickens for food is seldom the keeper's major goal.

From the beginning of the human/chicken relationship some 8,000 years ago, the main attraction wasn't meat, eggs, or profit—it was sport and entertainment. We're told that the first domestic chickens were fighting cocks. Cockfighting is still extremely popular in certain cultures. In ours, it's more acceptable to admire the birds' beauty and characteristics as set by certain standards of perfection, rather than their ferocity and bravery. Chickens have been shown at poultry shows in the United States since 1849, when more than 10,000 people admired 1,023 birds in the Public Gardens in Boston.

These are lovely hostas and lupines, but the chickens are even more beautiful!

(Photo: Brenda Carlson, New Auburn, Wisconsin)

The truth is, many people simply like to sit in the yard and watch their little flocks go about their business, which is generally catching bugs and taking dust baths. Some call it their "chicken TV." It's a relaxing way for busy modern people to connect with nature and simpler times. For many, their chickens are as beautiful and as satisfying as their flowers.

Four Reasons to Keep Chickens

Excluding the profit factor, there are four primary reasons to raise chickens: eggs, meat, exhibition, and just plain fun. For people with only a few birds, whether in town or in the country, fun and entertainment is the main draw.

It's true, all hens lay eggs, and all chickens have breasts, wings, and drumsticks. But some hens will lay an egg almost every day, while others might lay one once in a while and then quit. Some birds will provide a tasty chicken dinner in a matter of weeks, while others take months and still might not be toothsome, much less economical. Some chickens will perch on your shoulder and eat out of your hand, while others are as wild as owls. And as you might expect in a jack-of-all-trades category, multipurpose birds are masters of none—which doesn't mean they might not be ideal for you, if you, too, have multiple purposes. Then there are people who like their chickens big or small; black, white, red, or multicolored; with feathers growing on their feet or spiking out the tops of their heads like punk-rock stars. Choosing your first chickens can be a problem!

Some chickens have silky feathers, some have frizzled feathers, and some have feathery punk-rocker hair-dos. There's a chicken for everyone!

(Photo: Ann Mirek, Glendale, Wisconsin)

Most people have a hard time choosing their favorite breed of chicken. Maybe that's why there are so many mixed flocks, like this one.

(Photo: Natasha Tisdale, Saucier, Mississippi)

The Egg Chicken

The choice is not nearly as complicated for commercial chicken farmers. If they want to sell eggs, they select a breed that was genetically designed to lay as many eggs as possible with as little feed as possible, and is adaptable to living in a small cage (as little as 46.5 square inches in the United States, and 70 square inches in Canada).

The breed that best meets these demands is the White Leghorn. It's a small, lightweight bird that doesn't expend feed energy on body mass, or making meat. In addition, it lays a large egg for its size. Genetic tweaking has created many strains and hybrids of the breed—improvements, as far as profitability is concerned. If you want lots of eggs and nothing else, you might consider these specialized birds, too, although the old-fashioned purebred Leghorns, either white or brown, are more popular for home flocks.

Leghorns are rather common looking, excitable, more businesslike than personable, and in general, not as much fun to have around as some of the others, but they do have their fans.

Cocktail Conversation

In 1909, the average hen layed 83 eggs. By 2004, the average for commercial layers reached 260 eggs. The increase resulted from changes in genetics, feed, housing, and other management factors that transformed egg production from a small-farm enterprise to a highly industrialized agribusiness.

The Meat Chicken

If farmers want to sell broilers, they choose a fast-growing, meaty bird. The number-one choice is a White Rock–Cornish cross (a hybrid, or crossbreed), again with many different strains available. Although these larger birds do lay eggs, they don't lay as many as Leghorns, and they eat more feed per egg layed. Their *feed conversion ratio* is good for meat but not for eggs.

def•i•ni•tion

> **Feed conversion ratio** (FCR) is the amount of feed it takes to produce a pound of weight gain. For example, if a chicken gains a pound of body weight by eating 2 pounds of feed, the FCR is 1:2. For pigs, the FCR is commonly 1:4; for beef, 1:7 or 8. This is one reason chicken is cheaper than other meats.
>
> The typical hen eats 4 to 5 pounds of feed to produce a dozen eggs. This is also referred to as a feed conversion ratio. The more a hen eats to produce an egg, the more expensive her eggs are. Some homegrown eggs are *very* expensive.

Agribusiness pays close attention to feed conversion ratios because that's how they make money. They're counting fractions of pennies on hundreds of thousands or even millions of birds. Feed conversion ratios aren't nearly as important to someone with a few chickens in the backyard, but they should still be considered if economical egg production is important. It's a matter of both breed selection and management, so it's crucial to start with the right breed.

def•i•ni•tion

A **broiler** or **fryer** is a young meat–type chicken, usually about nine weeks old, weighing between 2½ and 3½ pounds. A **roaster** is a young meat–type chicken weighing 4 pounds or more. A **stewing chicken, hen,** or **fowl** is a mature female chicken, often the by-product of egg production, with tougher meat that is best cooked by stewing, or in soup.

If your main interest is fresh eggs, get a breed known for its egg-laying ability and efficiency, such as the White or Brown Leghorn for white eggs, the Rhode Island Red for brown-shelled eggs, or one of the hybrids now widely available and advertised as layers. (We'll talk more about breeds in Chapter 2 and eggshell colors in Chapter 5.) If you want meat, a Cornish-Rock cross is a good choice, although here again, there are many varieties and strains. If you want both eggs and meat from one breed, choose a so-called dual-purpose chicken such as the White Rock, Barred Rock, New Hampshire Red, or Wyandotte. None of these lay as well as the laying breeds, but they are meatier. They're not as meaty as the commercial meat breeds, but they lay better. For the backyard farmer or homesteader with a few birds who wants a little of everything, they might be ideal. However, don't think you can have a hen lay eggs for a few years and then become a chicken dinner. There's a big difference between a *broiler* or *fryer,* a *roaster,* and a *stewing hen.*

The Fancy Chicken

Then there are those chicken raisers who are perfectly satisfied with fancy or exotic breeds, or even bantams, that are prized for neither meat nor eggs and yet produce both. You might enjoy their color, shape, size, or personality.

If you get serious about exhibiting chickens in competitive shows, even such details as the size of a comb and the angle of a tail are more important than the number of eggs layed or the amount of meat produced. Then you'll become involved in the technicalities of breeding for those desirable traits. This means you'll have to study the American Poultry Association's *American Standard of Perfection* to display your birds by the APA rules or the similar standards of the American Bantam Association. You'll also need to study the birds you'll see at the poultry shows in order to know what a good one looks like. And, of course, it requires knowledge of genetics, nutrition, and general good management in order to breed a champion. It's challenging and entertaining.

The Brahma chicken was a sensation in America and Europe when it was first introduced from China in the 1840s. Known as the Brahma Pootra, Chittagong, and other exotic names, it was a major participant in (or victim of) the "Hen Fever" of the 1850s, which has been compared to the Tulip Mania of the 1600s.

(Photo: Chelsea Disher, Germantown, New York)

The Backyard Chicken

Then there is the chicken sometimes referred to as "pet," or "urban," although neither is necessarily accurate. These chickens have taken the country by storm in the past few years. They seldom produce meat, being more likely to get a decent burial after a natural death, normally at age 8 to 10. Most of them do lay eggs, but that's often just an excuse to justify keeping them, not really an economic consideration. They never get to strut their stuff on a show table in front of a poultry judge.

Fresh, homegrown, cage-free eggs might be the impetus for keeping most of these small flocks. But the truth is, after a while, most of these chickens are kept for the pleasure of their company, even when they stop laying.

It's not easy to pin down the attraction, maybe because there are so many. Some people see their small flocks as a sign of independence and self-sufficient living. Others are striking a blow for animal rights, eating eggs that don't come from the caged hens they consider mistreated. Undoubtedly some chickens are nothing but lawn ornaments—perhaps a poor man's peacock. Gardeners appreciate the manure, and recyclers like the way chickens turn table scraps into eggs and compost. No matter what the main attraction is, chickens are simply beautiful birds that brighten their surroundings with brilliant color and cheerful chatter.

But it doesn't take long for a chicken to become a member of the family, just like a dog or cat. Particularly when allowed to range free, so its chickenness can be exercised, seen, and appreciated, a chicken is an entertaining, fascinating creature.

There truly is a chicken for everyone. One of your first duties is to decide why you want to raise chickens, to be sure you start out with the right kind. But before we get that far, should you be raising poultry at all?

Is Raising Chickens Right for Me?

Not everyone is able, or suited to, keeping animals of any kind. You need a certain level of commitment in order to be entrusted with a living creature that's dependent on you for its very existence, as a confined chicken is. You need the dedication required to provide clean water, fresh food, and sanitation every day of the year, whether or not you're in the mood. You must be responsible, attuned to the needs of your chickens, your family, and the neighbors. And, of course, you need the proper location and facilities.

In the recent past, if no one complained about a neighbor's chickens, there was little concern about laws and ordinances. Although this attitude is still common, an increasing number of cities and towns are paying attention to the burgeoning interest in urban poultry, very often coming out in their favor. Most of these ordinances prohibit roosters, regulate numbers, and specify distances between coops and property lines or houses. Some are so ridiculously stringent they make keeping chickens impossible, and others outlaw them bluntly. But in the main, chickens are gaining some respect. If this affects or concerns you, check with your city or town clerk to find out what the local situation is. (Also find more in Chapter 9.)

Caring for living animals is a 365-day-a-year responsibility, so you must have a capable and willing stand-in for those times when it would be impossible for you to fulfill your duties personally. Not everyone is as dedicated as the lady who insisted on feeding her chickens even on her wedding day and had her picture taken doing it—in her wedding gown!

How Much Does It Cost?

Compared with other livestock and pets, chickens are dirt cheap. Day-old chicks can be had for $2 or $3 each, depending on breed and quantity. In certain times and places you can find grown birds for not much more, although normally you should expect to pay the chick price plus the feed and labor that has gone into it.

"Chicken feed" is an old term referring to an insignificant amount of money. Feed prices vary widely and sometimes wildly, and "cheap" is relative, so let's just say it doesn't cost a bundle to feed a chicken. A 50-pound bag of feed in my area today runs from $8 to $10, with organic feed about twice that. Since you'll have to find a local source anyway, it's easy to check on the current local price before you get your birds.

Equipment is minimal, as we'll see in a moment. For most urban chicken projects, the greatest expense is almost certainly housing, mainly because some people make it so. If you have a structure that will serve as a suitable chicken shelter, your cost might be nil; if you hire an architect and contractor to build a chicken coop that complements your mansion, well, that's your option.

> **Cacklings**
>
> Chickens will forage for bugs, seeds, and other food, in certain locations and situations. Since they are omnivores and eat people food, they can be fed table scraps. We'll examine feeds in more detail in Chapter 11, but for most people reading this book, commercially prepared feeds are the easiest and most economical route, and the best to start with.

A bird in the hand is worth ... as much or as little as you're willing to spend!

(Photo: Don Archer, Marietta, Ohio)

As with anything, costs can vary, from almost nothing to small fortunes. It's possible to buy hatching eggs for more than $50 a dozen, 40 pounds of organic feed for $25, and a ready-made coop for $2,000 and up. That makes eggs pricey.

However, *The People's Farm and Stock Cyclopedia*, published in 1885, suggested that chickens started in spring could roost in trees during the summer; like those in Key West, Kauai, and Grand Cayman, they don't need any housing at all. In the fall and winter they could be kept in a sod house, the author stated.

You might not want to go to that extreme, but as a general rule, keeping a few chickens is not a large expense, and if you do everything right, the eggs might actually pay for themselves.

How Much Work Is Involved?

Chickens that don't roost in trees and run wild do require daily attention, but not much more than a cat or dog. They must be fed and watered. One difference is that with chickens, you might have to pick up an egg now and then, but how much trouble can that be?

You'll want to clean and sanitize feeders and waterers once a week, especially in hot weather. You'll have to clean their coop once a week or once a year, depending on the design. We discuss that in Chapter 4. Basically, you can count on spending several minutes a day caring for your flock. You'll probably want to spend much more than that just enjoying their company, and most of the time none of it will be considered "labor."

Building a coop and outdoor run takes time and effort as well as cash, of course. The amount is largely up to you, but this is a one-time project.

How Much Space Do I Need?

Chickens require very little room. I mentioned earlier that some commercial laying hens exist in cages with a paltry 46.5 square inches of space. This obviously is not what you, as a backyarder, have in mind. But even with more pleasant and humane surroundings, a few hens don't need much room. Three or four square feet per bird will suffice for a house, and even less in mild climates. Although they would be delighted to have access to the whole world—and you should provide as much outdoor space as your situation allows—there are ways to keep birds happy and healthy with just a few square feet, with a moveable pen and other clever ideas. This is a case where more is better, up to a point, but you don't need an estate or acreage to enjoy keeping a few hens.

How Do I Get Started?

Dozens of stories exist about how people got their first chickens. Over the years, many backyard flocks have been started with chicks adopted from school science projects. A few weeks later these, along with dyed Easter chicks that have also outgrown their cuteness, are foisted on somebody who lives in the country, "has room" for a few chickens, and doesn't have the guts to refuse a gift. More than a few old hens have been picked up along the highway, presumably having escaped from a truck delivering them to the soup factory. Unfortunately, it is now possible to find chickens at some pet shelters.

A better way to get started is by deciding what kind of chickens you want and finding out where they are available. We have already seen that the first step in decision-making is determining which of the four main chicken functions interests you most—eggs, meat, show, or fun. For the typical backyarder, deciding on function is easy compared to deciding on a particular breed, or even color, size, or shape! This is no doubt one reason so many small flocks are "mixed," with birds of various breeds. The owners either like them all, or just couldn't make up their minds.

Which Breed?

We'll examine some of the breed options in Chapter 2, but after that decision has been made, you have to find the birds. If you have your heart set on a specific breed that's quite rare, that might not be easy. Conversely, a popular breed might be sold out by the time you decide to place your order. You will no doubt want to try different breeds in the future, but plan on being flexible at first.

The Silver Spangled Spitzhauben originated in Switzerland and is their national bird, but it's very rare in the United States.

(Photo: Deanna Stinnett, Jefferson, Texas)

Chicks, Pullets, or Full-Grown?

Likewise, your choice of the age to start with might be limited by what's available, especially if you're in a hurry (and who isn't, after the decision to get chickens is made?). Normally, most chicks are hatched in the spring, so you have a limited window of opportunity to make your purchase. It follows that pullets (young females, or hens) are most widely available in summer and fall. Traditionally, chickens of this age weren't even an option. Now some entrepreneurs are raising chicks to sell as pullets, but this still isn't common. It's best to plan on starting with chicks in spring or early summer.

Go online or write for a few hatchery catalogs. (Find their names and addresses in Appendix C.) You'll want to do this anyway, sooner or later, just for the beautiful pictures and to learn more about different breeds, as well as to see what's available. Most people get their first chickens by mail-order.

If you want to start with older chickens, purchased locally, and you live in an area where chicken fever is running high—where everybody knows somebody who raises chickens—it will be easy to find both advice and birds. Just ask around.

If you don't know a soul who has chickens, find a feed mill or store that sells poultry feeds. (This is sage advice anyway in areas where feed might be hard to obtain; be sure you have a source of feed before you get the birds!) Feed dealers should be able to tell you who is buying their products.

The 4-H agent at your County Extension Office can tell you if anybody is raising chickens as a 4-H project. Not surprisingly, this is becoming very popular and widespread.

Fox Alert

The question is sure to come up: Do I need a rooster in order to get eggs? No. Look for a more complete, technical, and interesting answer in Chapter 5.

The Least You Need to Know

- ◆ Chickens require little space and are relatively inexpensive and easy to raise.
- ◆ Chickens are raised for eggs, meat, show, and fun.
- ◆ Most chicks come from commercial hatcheries and are sold by mail-order.
- ◆ A hen can lay eggs without a rooster.

Chapter 2

The Family Tree

In This Chapter

- ◆ Not all chickens are created equal
- ◆ Know the breeds
- ◆ A bit about bantams
- ◆ Twenty-four billion, and going extinct?

To most people, a chicken is just a big white bird. Or even worse, it's something a Kentucky colonel fries by the millions.

But to those in the know, so many different kinds of chickens abound that they need a serious way of keeping track of them all. Here's how chickens are classified.

Classes of Chickens

If your last bout with a biology class was recent enough that you can still remember some of it, you might recall how living things are classified: you know, that textbook stuff about Kingdoms and so forth. Chickens are in the *Animalia* kingdom. Then there is Phylum (chickens are *Chordata*), Subphylum (*Vertebrata*), and in the bird Class (*Aves*). Our feathered friends

Fox Alert

Don't confuse the biology textbook "Class" with the "classes" the American Poultry Association assigns chickens to. There is no connection.

def•i•ni•tion

A **class** of chickens is a group that shares similar attributes such as body type. A **breed** is a group within a class with special characteristics passed on by inheritance or genetics. A **variety** is a subdivision within a breed based on minor distinctions, such as comb type or feather color. A **strain** denotes related birds within a variety, sharing a common ancestry.

are all of these, but there's more. They're in the Order *Galliformes*, or chickenlike birds, which distinguishes them from more than two dozen other orders of birds.

Finally, we get down to what you and I could simply call a "chicken," except that we want to know a lot more about it. So we (or rather, the American Poultry Association, Inc., or APA) further break them down into conveniently recognized *classes*. This is where it starts to make sense, at least so far as practical chicken-raising is concerned.

There are 11 classes of chickens. Most of them indicate where the bird originated. When we're familiar with the classes, just knowing which one a chicken belongs to tells us a great deal about the bird.

Then each class is divided into *breeds*, which strain out the differences with an even finer mesh. And finally, the breed *variety* takes it down to the *n*th degree that tells us practically everything there is to know about any chicken except its family background—which we learn from the *strain*.

The American Class

One class is the American, describing birds that were developed in their present form in the United States and Canada. This class includes such favorites as the Rhode Island Red, a cross between the Red Malay Game, Leghorn, and Asiatic native stock and recognized as a distinct breed by the American Poultry Association in 1904. There are two varieties of that breed: the single comb and the rose comb. Today, many strains of Rhode Island Red also exist and are used for commercial egg production.

The Barred Plymouth Rock was included in the very first edition of the American Poultry Association's *American Standard of Excellence* (later the *American Standard of Perfection*) in 1874. The white variety, now often referred to simply as a White Rock, followed in 1888. There are now seven varieties of this breed.

The White Rock is a classic American breed. Today it's used as the female side of the commercial broiler production Rock-Cornish cross, the most numerous bird in the world.

(Photo: Melissa Godfrey, Elizabethtown, Kentucky)

The Wyandotte breed originated in New York with several names, until it was admitted to the Standard in 1883 as the Silver Laced Wyandotte. Its parentage is unknown, but the Golden Laced Wyandotte that appeared in Wisconsin in 1880 was a cross of a Silver Laced Wyandotte hen with a Partridge Cochin/Brown Leghorn. These were followed by the White, Black, Buff, Partridge, Silver Pencilled, and Columbian varieties, joined by the Blue in 1977—one of the youngest varieties in the Standard.

Other well-known breeds in the American Class include Plymouth Rock, Dominique, and Java, which was named for the island of Java but was greatly modified here before being admitted to the Standard in 1883, making it an American. Buckeyes are from Ohio, naturally, and the only breed developed by a woman.

The Lamona is interesting because, unlike the breeds that were developed by fanciers, it originated at the U.S. Government Experiment Station at Beltsville, Maryland. This cross of Silver Gray Dorkings, White Plymouth Rocks, and Single Comb White Leghorns produced a general-purpose fowl for both meat and eggs— in 1933, when specialization was becoming the order of the day.

Cocktail Conversation

Even though women were the traditional poultry caretakers, most of their concerns were more practical, and breeding for the fancy was left to well-to-do men with nothing better to do.

The Chantecler, the first breed from Canada, was also a government-originated bird, from the Oka Agricultural Institute in Quebec. It, too, was a "general-purpose fowl" but designed for the Canadian climate, as early as 1918.

The Asiatic Class

The Asiatic Class was represented at the first poultry show in the United States in 1874 by both the Light and Dark Brahma, which earlier had been called Chittagongs, Gray Shanghais, and Brahma Pootras. These large exotic birds (cocks weigh 12 pounds), with their exotic names, arrived in New England with the Cochins soon after Chinese ports were first opened to world trade in the early 1840s, and quickly created the "hen fever" that took much of the country by storm.

Light Brahmas are very large but gentle birds from the Orient that played a large role in the "hen fever" of the 1850s in both England and the United States.

(Photo: Amos Haley, Orville, Ohio)

Chinese Shanghai fowl, later called Cochins, arrived in England about the same time and created a similar sensation. Although a bit lighter than the Brahma, the Cochin's profusion of long, soft plumage makes it look even more massive and unlike any chicken seen in England or America before.

Cochins were called Chinese Shanghai fowl when they were introduced to Western poultry fanciers in 1845. Their profuse soft feathering created a sensation and made poultry fanciers out of many ordinary people. These Cochins are of the bantam variety.

(Photo: Melissa Holcomb, Broken Arrow, Oklahoma)

The nine varieties of Cochins are Buff, Partridge, White, Black, Silver Laced, Golden Laced, Blue, Brown, and Barred. The third and smallest member of the Asiatic Class is the Langshan.

The English Class

The English Class includes one of the oldest breeds, the Dorking, said to have arrived in Britain with Julius Caesar. This is one of the five-toed breeds; four-toed chickens are more common. Other breeds in the English Class are Redcaps, Orpingtons, and Sussex. However, this Class also contains the Cornish, which has contributed to the commercially produced meat birds of today and, therefore, is the most numerous bird in the world, being raised by the billions. Another member is the Australorp, an Australian derivative of the Black Orpington, bred for egg production.

The Mediterranean Class

Next is the Mediterranean Class, which includes the Leghorn breed and its 16 varieties, many of which are designated by comb type (single or rose). Like the Cornish, the Leghorn has proliferated through its production crosses, becoming the premier egg-laying bird in the world. The breed originated in Italy, but most of the subvarieties originated in America, England, and Denmark.

Other Mediterranean breeds are the White-Faced Black Spanish, Andalusian, Minorca, and Catalana, all of which originated in Spain. The Ancona came from Italy, and the Silician Buttercup, so-called because of its cup-shaped comb, actually did originate in Sicily.

Poultry often provides a life-long hobby and interest. At 13, Brandon Rux is already a five-year-veteran of chicken raising and showing. Here he displays his five-month-old Black Australorp.

(Photo: Kelly Rux, Oconomowoc, Wisconsin)

The Continental Class

The Continental Class has three divisions: Northern European, Polish, and French.

The Northern European Class includes Barnevelders, Hamburgs, Campines, Lakenvelders, and Welsummers, the latter two being prized for their dark brown eggs.

Polish is a class by itself with 11 varieties—and its distinctive crest. Also present in the Houdan and Crevecour, the large crest is due partly to feathers but mainly to a large knob on the skull and cavernous nostrils.

The French include Houdans, Crevecours, Faverolles, and La Fleche. Anyone who knows a tad about language might be excused for assuming that La Fleche has something to do with feathers; in reality, it's the name of a town in the La Sarthe Valley of France, where these birds have been raised for many years and have earned a reputation for their fine meat.

Several breeds feature crests, including the Polish, Houdan, and Crevecour. This is a White Polish Bantam.

(Photo: Brenda Ernst, Hamersville, Ohio)

You'd think this would be enough variety to satisfy anybody, but we're not even close to being finished. Dip into the *American Standard of Perfection* and you learn about both Modern and Old English Games; Sumatras, Malays, Cubalayas, and Aseels; and the long-tailed Phoenix and Yokohama. You see Sultans, Frizzles, and Naked Necks, and of course, you've heard of "the Easter egg chickens," the Araucana and Ameraucana.

In a rare bit of candor, the American Standard of Perfection *says, "Frizzles are one of our odd breeds."* Indeed!

(Photo: Penelope O'Neill, Los Gatos, California)

But then, the APA recognizes only a fraction of the more than 300 breeds of chickens found worldwide. And it pays no attention to the last tip of the last branch of the family tree, the strain. Many strains have been developed and named, especially for commercial purposes. You might encounter such names as DeKalb, Hyline, Shaver, and Babcock. In industrial factory farming, some poor chickens don't even rate real names: they're simply known as strain w37 or some such.

Bantams, Briefly

First there was a town in Indonesia named Bantam. Some very small chickens that supposedly originated there were soon called bantams, or banties for short. Before long, anything small could be called a bantam, especially if it was feisty, such as a bantamweight boxer. Cockadoodledom is filled with trickle-down stories like this, showing just how much chickens have infiltrated our lives, even our language.

Silkies are very unusual and popular bantams.

(Photo: Matthew Phillips, Thornwood, New York)

Bantam chickens are usually about one fourth or one fifth the size and weight of their larger brethren. They're not exact miniatures of large breeds because their proportions are different, and not all bantams have large counterparts. Some have colors and shapes not seen in standard-size chickens, earning them the title "flower garden of the poultry world." This alone makes them worthy of consideration for the backyarder.

According to the APA, there is so much interest in bantams that many poultry shows have more bantams than large birds.

Although their eggs are small—it takes about three banty eggs to equal one large egg—they are relatively large for the size of the bird. Bantam weight varies by breed, but it's often around 2 pounds, or close to the size of the so-called "Cornish game hens" found in the supermarket. Bantams are economical to feed, making both eggs and meat worthwhile.

Cacklings

Bantams obviously take up less room, too. Putting it all together, bantam chickens can be a very good choice if you have limited space.

The Disappearing Breeds

With 24 billion chickens in the world and about 350 breeds, you might think there's little chance of a chicken becoming extinct. That's not the case.

The American Livestock Breeds Conservancy (ALBC), which monitors livestock populations in the United States, currently has 19 breeds of chickens on its "Critical" list. This means there are fewer than 500 breeding birds, with 5 or fewer primary breeding flocks (50 birds or more), and that the breed is globally endangered.

In addition to the Critical list, ALBC also considers 7 breeds "Threatened," places 10 on the "Watch" list, 6 on the "Recovering," and 12 on what it calls its "Study" list.

Many people who are not only chicken lovers but are also against factory farming and in favor of diversity, naturally feel compelled to take one of these rare breeds under their wing to help preserve the genetics. Diversified genetics, in both plants and animals, are of great importance for economic as well as aesthetic reasons. For more information, visit ALBC at www.albc-usa.org.

The Least You Need to Know

◆ The American Poultry Association divides chickens into 11 classes.

◆ There are an estimated 350 different chicken breeds in the world.

◆ Bantams are about one fourth the size of regular chickens.

◆ Several dozen breeds are in danger of extinction.

Chapter 3

Getting Started

In This Chapter

- ◆ How nature does it
- ◆ The modern way
- ◆ Brooding chicks
- ◆ The laying house

You can start raising poultry in several ways. When you realize that neither the chicken nor the egg comes first, that it's just one continuous cycle, you can decide to jump in at any point on that cycle. To help you make that decision, in this chapter I tell you how the cycle works, what's involved at each step, and where you might best join the fun.

The Natural Way

Chickens don't need any human help to live and reproduce. The feral fowl of Key West and Hawaii are good examples, but many hobby farms are also homes to very independent, self-sufficient poultry.

A hen and rooster mate. The hen lays fertile eggs. She incubates them for 21 days. They hatch, grow up, and the cycle starts all over again. Chickens are simple. Humans make the process complicated.

The main problem, for humans, is that for the 21 days the hen is setting, and for several weeks afterward, while she is being a mother hen to her chicks, she doesn't lay any eggs. Agribusiness egg producers don't like that. If she's not laying, they aren't making any money. So the mothering instinct has been bred out of commercial laying hens.

A setting hen is an easy target for predators, and her eggs are even more vulnerable: snakes, possums, and skunks are among the many creatures who savor eggs. This factor also cuts into profits. Human ingenuity has overcome these obstacles by mechanizing the chicken-rearing process. Most of the 24 billion chickens on Earth are no longer natural creatures, but freaks: they have mutated genes, and they're hatched by machines.

> **Cocktail Conversation**
>
> I once got into trouble by writing a direct-mail ad for *Countryside* magazine with the screaming headline, "Hatch Chicks in Your Bra!" That didn't sit well with a certain segment of the population (and even garnered a mention in a *Time* magazine article on direct marketing), but it was based on several true stories told to me by readers.
>
> A Peace Corps Volunteer in Africa wanted to upgrade a village's chickens. She was frustrated by snakes snapping up the chicks as soon as they hatched under the hens. With no incubator, she decided to gather the eggs on the twentieth day, keeping them warm on her bosom. It worked. Another woman reported doing the same with an ostrich egg, worth $1,000 at that time, when the power went out.
>
> Fortunately, chicken people were more intrigued than offended by these stories, and the mailing was a huge success.

Disrupted egg production was recognized as an economic problem by both Chinese and Egyptians as early as 4,000 years ago. Their solution was artificial incubation. The Egyptians developed huge wood-fired ovens. The Chinese used composting manure as a heat source.

The Mechanical Way

That ancient technology was lost for thousands of years. It wasn't until around 1750 that a Frenchman constructed a wood-fired incubator that apparently worked. The first American kerosene incubator was patented in 1843. An electric hatching machine was introduced in 1923, but since electricity on farms was rare until the 1930s, kerosene incubators and *brooders* were still common in the 1940s. And, of course, chickens continued to do their own thing without human interference, until humans interfered in a new way and bred the mothering instinct out of them.

def•i•ni•tion

A **brooder** is a heated space or structure used to raise young fowl. A *brood* is a number of young animals, especially birds produced at one hatching, and cared for at one time. A *broody* hen is one that sits on a nest of eggs to hatch them to produce a brood. She then *broods* her chicks by hovering over them, often covering them with her wings.

Today, a commercial incubator can hatch upward of 100,000 eggs at a time with perfectly controlled heat, humidity, egg turning, and sanitation.

However, you can also buy or build an incubator to hatch as few as three eggs and get your start from the beginning, as it were. You'll find a good selection of small and inexpensive table-top incubators that can hold a few dozen eggs. Some even have automatic turning systems. Naturally you need some hatching eggs, and finding them isn't as easy or as cheap as it was in the good old days. Some hatching eggs of rare breeds can cost $50 or more per dozen.

Fox Alert

Do not use store-bought eggs in an incubator. Commercial laying hens never even see a rooster; the eggs are not fertile; and they will not hatch.

The simplest (and cheapest) incubators are termed still-air, as opposed to forced-air. Any type will work as long it meets the four requirements of incubation:

♦ A steady temperature of 102°F to 103°F in a still-air machine, and 99.5°F in a forced-air one

♦ A 60 percent relative humidity, increased to 70 percent the last three days of the hatch

♦ Exercise, in the form of turning the eggs an odd number of times a day from the second to the eighteenth day

♦ Ventilation, to supply fresh air to the embryos

Don't expect 100 percent of the eggs to hatch. All too often, none of them do. Improper humidity is one of the main reasons for losses in artificially incubated chicks. If the humidity isn't high enough, the membrane sticks to the chick, preventing its turning inside the egg. The chick then has trouble orienting itself inside the egg and might not be able to *pip* the shell. An additional source of moisture, such as a damp sponge, should be placed in the incubator on the eighteenth day.

Other reasons for poor hatches—from either an incubator or a broody hen—include infertile eggs; old eggs; weak parent stock; improper care of eggs; shell contamination; humidity or ventilation; and infrequent turning.

def•i•ni•tion

To **pip** is to break through an eggshell in hatching.

The **egg tooth** is a small, sharp cranial protuberance the chick uses to cut a hole in an eggshell so it can hatch.

On or about the twenty-first day the chick will use its *egg tooth* to pip the shell, and it's "born." This is exhausting work and can take several hours. Some chicks don't survive the ordeal. You might be tempted to help a struggling chick, but in most cases if the chick isn't strong enough to hatch by itself, it won't be strong enough to survive.

The chicks can be left in the incubator until all are hatched and dry. Then remove them to the brooder. Clean and sanitize the incubator.

Cacklings

You might wonder about starting your flock by buying some eggs and a broody hen—that is, a hen inclined to sit and hatch eggs, rather than lay more of them. However, a broody hen that's moved to a new location isn't likely to remain broody and the eggs won't hatch. You're better off starting with day-old chicks.

Breaking through an eggshell is hard work!

(Photo: Rick Bushey, Chicken Little's Poultry Haven, Wasilla, Alaska)

It should be apparent by now that hatching eggs in an incubator is no stroll in the park. It certainly isn't as simple as bringing home live chicks. And considering the expense of the machine and hatching eggs—and the risk of failure—incubator hatching is not nearly as cheap as it might seem. If you want or can have only hens, what will you do with the male chicks—after feeding them for the several weeks it will take before you'll know what sex they are? You might want to try hatching eggs after you gain some poultry experience (and if you have a rooster), but it's not the usual or recommended way to start a backyard flock.

It's much better to jump into the cycle after the chicks come out of the incubator and are ready to brood.

Fox Alert

Don't expect to be able to determine the sex of a day-old chick by looking at it. You won't know what sex newborn chicks are because the sexual organs are inside the body, and chicks don't have the combs and feathers that later can identify their sex. Secondary sex characteristics won't show up for four to six weeks.

Mail-Order Chicks

The most common way to start raising chickens is with day-old chicks from a commercial hatchery. In rural areas, many feed and farm supply stores offer chicks for sale in the spring, but you'll find a much wider choice from the mail-order hatcheries. Don't worry: chicks have been shipped by mail for generations. Sears & Roebuck used to be a major supplier. Today a large selection of hatcheries are catering to the backyard hobbyist, offering many different breeds. Some are listed in Appendix C. Obviously, looking at the catalog descriptions and color pictures and making wish lists is a big part of the fun, but many of the catalogs are also educational, so be sure to order several.

You can order chicks as pullets (young females, or hens), cockerels (young males, or roosters), or straight run (a 50–50 mix, just as they come from the incubator and the hen). If you can't have or don't want roosters, being able to order just pullets is an obvious advantage.

Cocktail Conversation

Sexing day-old chicks is not easy, except for the few so-called sex-links (chickens developed by crossing certain breeds, resulting in chicks whose sex is evidenced by color, or sometimes by feather development, at hatching). For the majority, vent sexing is required. Vent sexing involves examining the genitals and is an extremely specialized skill. It originated in Japan in the 1920s to eliminate the cockerels of laying breeds before spending time and money on brooding them, only to destroy them later. For many years afterward, most chick sexers were Japanese, sometimes reportedly earning thousands of dollars a day in the United States.

Chicks can be shipped by mail because they don't require food for 48 hours after hatching; they are still living off the nutriments in the yolk.

However, they do require warmth. One reason most hatcheries won't ship fewer than 25 chicks at a time is that larger numbers provide more body heat. This used to be a problem for backyarders who only wanted, or were only allowed to have, three or four chickens. Today, in a nod to this new class of small-scale customer, some hatcheries are finding ways to lower the limit, in some cases down to three.

The Four Principles of Chick Brooding

Brooding chicks is simple and easy for the backyarder. Heat, water, feed, and sanitation are the four principles of successful chick brooding.

Heat

To provide heat for a few chicks, all you need is a cardboard box (the brooder) with a light bulb.

A chick should have at least ½ square foot of space until it's four weeks old, and about 1 square foot from four to eight weeks. This means an 18 × 24-inch box, such as reams of paper come in, could accommodate three chicks. A 24 × 36-inch box will hold five or six chicks for a month. They can be kept warm with a gooseneck lamp and a 75-watt bulb if the room is reasonably warm. If you use a hanging reflector lamp, be sure it has a wire guard over the bulb to keep it from touching flammable materials, and hang it from a chain, not by the cord, for safety.

Test the heat source well before the chicks arrive. Ideal temperature is 95°F at chick height, or about 2 inches off the floor. Raise or lower the lamp to achieve that and check to be certain the temperature is maintained. Lower the heat about 5°F per week by raising the lamp, until the brooder temperature matches the outdoor temperature.

Ground corncobs, wood chips, peat moss, and chopped straw all make good bedding, or litter. It should be 2 to 3 inches deep. It's common to spread newspaper on top of the litter for the first few days, with feed sprinkled on the paper. This prevents the chicks from eating litter at first, and helps teach them how to eat. However, anything slick or slippery, such as newsprint, can lead to "spraddle legs," especially in broilers or heavy breeds. This causes the chicks to sprawl, and is usually fatal. You can crinkle the paper well so it's not smooth, but a better alternative today is to use paper toweling. Don't leave any paper on the litter for more than a day or so.

Not many things are as cute as fluffy chicks.

(Photo: Rosemary Stockwell, Pollach, Louisiana)

Construct a draft shield for your brooder. In large brooders this is a foot-high cardboard or metal circular enclosure placed under the heat lamp, not so much to deflect drafts, but to keep the chicks from piling up in the corners and to keep them near the heat source at first. In a small box, just tape pieces of cardboard in the corners to round them off. The ring should be large enough to enable the chicks to move to a cooler area if they become overheated. It can be removed in a week or so, and the chicks can move closer to or farther from the heat, as they wish. Chicks feather out better when they have a cooler area to exercise in.

Give some thought to where you'll locate the brooder. It doesn't have to be in a heated space, but if it's chilly, pay much closer attention to the lamp and drafts. Good ventilation is important, but avoid drafts. The brooder obviously should be well protected from cats, dogs, and other predators. And chicks create a lot of dust, especially as their feathers grow; they produce a kind of talc to lubricate the process, and it gets into everything. Don't plan on keeping chicks where that dust will be a problem.

Water

Furnish the brooder with an inexpensive plastic waterer that fits on a canning or mayonnaise jar, and a small feeder, both available from a farm supply store.

Give your chicks water only—no feed—for the first hour. Drinking is more important, and feed will only distract them. As each chick is removed from the shipping box, dip its beak into the water to make sure it knows how to find the water. (Warm water is preferred; chicks don't like cold water.) A 1-quart jar of water should serve up to a dozen chicks, but keep an eye on the waterer. It must be clean, and never let it run out. It also should not be too deep. Chicks can drown in 1½ inches of water. If your waterer is deeper than that, add pebbles or colorful marbles, which also attract the chicks' attention and encourage drinking.

Getting chicks to drink is your first task.

(Photo: Jamie Ayers, Vienna, Ohio)

Feed

Day-old chicks need a starter feed containing 20 percent protein.

Several types of small feeders for chicks are available. Your choice is a matter of personal preference, or at first, perhaps, is limited to what's readily available. (Truth be told, many people with a few birds use egg cartons cut in two.) The rule is 30 linear feet of feeder space per 100 birds, but with just a few chicks, space is seldom a problem. Don't fill a feeder more than half full, to avoid excessive waste.

You should, of course, have a feed source lined up, probably a feed or farm supply store. Be sure they have the three types you'll need: chick starter; grower (for meat birds) or pullet developer (for layers); and for laying hens, a layer ration. These feeds are formulated for the nutritional needs of the birds at each stage of development.

Feeds are available as pellets, crumbles, or a finely ground mash. In most cases you'll have to take whatever you can get. This is not likely to include "organic" feed unless there is a local demand and a local supplier willing to meet that demand. Organic feeds are becoming more common and will no doubt become more widely available as demand increases, but we discuss this more later. (If feed is a major issue with you, check out Chapter 11.)

Sanitation

Sanitation involves keeping the litter clean and dry, and thoroughly cleaning the feeder and waterer. Stir the litter often to keep it from crusting, and change it when necessary, especially around the waterer. Clean the waterer daily and disinfect it at least once a week. Use a bleach solution—an ounce of bleach (2 tablespoons) to a gallon of warm (75°) water—and rinse thoroughly afterward.

A healthy chick.

(Photo: Jill Peck, Brant, Michigan)

Watch for Problems

Along with tending to the four principles, your other task is to closely observe the chicks. That's not difficult, since they're far more entertaining than most television shows or computer games! If they huddle close together and chirp loudly, they're cold. If they're panting, they're too hot. Make any necessary adjustments (by raising or lowering the heat source) so they chirp quietly and peacefully, and you'll know they are warm and content.

Problems are rare with small flocks that are well cared for, but there are several you should at least be aware of, just in case.

Spraddle leg, mentioned earlier, is a condition generally associated with heavy breeds, especially the Rock-Cornish cross, and slippery surfaces. If you catch it soon enough and eliminate the cause, the birds might recover.

Some chicks are afflicted with "pasting," or fecal matter that accumulates on the down around the vent. Causes might be too high or too low a temperature, or poor nutrition. This matter must be removed, carefully, without tearing the chick's tender skin, or it will harden, and the chick will die. It might be necessary to moisten it in order to remove it.

Occasionally, especially as they grow, chicks will pick on each other. It often starts on toes or emerging feathers. This behavior usually indicates that they are too crowded or warm, or lacking proper diet or ventilation. If correcting any of these deficiencies doesn't help—and it might not, after the bad habit has started—try adding a distraction such as a piece of sod or a handful of grass. In more extreme cases, cutting down on light or using a red bulb in a heat lamp should help, but be aware that birds won't eat properly without sufficient light. Bloodied birds should be removed and isolated, or they will be pecked to death.

> **Cocktail Conversation**
>
> In commercial flocks, chicks are usually debeaked, meaning as much as a quarter of their beaks are cut off. They can eat prepared feeds but cannot peck each other to death or forage.

Beyond the Brooder

The brooding stage will be over by the time the birds are 10 weeks old. They'll be ready to go outside into the chicken coop you have prepared (after reading Chapter 4).

It will be another 12 to 14 weeks before you can expect the first egg, but for all practical purposes they can now be considered adults, or at least teenagers.

If you buy started pullets or fully grown hens, the coop is where you'll begin. You can skip not only the incubator, but also the brooder, heat lamp, and chick-size feeder and water fount.

Note that at 10 weeks, a chick will have eaten about 10 pounds of feed (depending on size and breed, of course). The seller will want to recover the cost of that feed, plus enough to cover losses and other expenses such as litter, and no doubt a bit for labor. Started chicks cost more than day-old chicks, for good reason.

At this point each bird needs at least 3 square feet of coop space (some ordinances specify 4), plus a yard or run. Use regular, full-size feeders, allowing 4 to 5 linear inches of space per bird. An inch or so of watering space will be adequate.

Cacklings

Feeders come in several types. I like the hanging, or tube type (which look a lot like water founts). They come in sizes ranging from 12- to 50-pound capacities, but don't provide more than the birds can clean up in a day or two. They can be raised off the floor so the hens' scratching doesn't fill the feed trough area with litter, and they can be adjusted to any height convenient for the birds to reach.

If you use feed troughs, only fill them a third to half full, to reduce waste. Hanging feeders hold more feed, using gravity to fill the trough portion, but these, too, should be adjusted to limit the feed available and susceptible to waste. Do your best to keep wild birds, such as sparrows, as well as rats and mice, away from the feed. Windows should be screened. Store all feed in metal garbage cans with tight lids, and clean up any spills.

When and Where to Find Chickens

Chicks are generally available only in spring. It follows that started pullets are available only in summer. Mature birds are available anytime, but more are for sale in fall, when people don't want to have to overwinter them. This means that if you want birds *now*, you'll probably have to take what's available right now. If it's June, and you demand chicks of a certain breed, you might have to wait until next spring. (But order early, before they're sold out!)

Chickens are sold at shows, swap meets, and small-animal auctions. It's wise to be wary of such sales. Even if the birds are healthy, they might have been exposed to disease where many birds from different sources are gathered. It's much better for a beginner to buy from someone who is willing and able to provide support and advice—someone you know and can visit. Ideally, you can look over the seller's birds and premises when you buy.

The Least You Need to Know

- Chickens are simple; humans make raising them complicated.

- Chickens and eggs revolve in an endless cycle, and you can jump in anywhere.

- Hatching eggs in an incubator is not the easiest or cheapest way to start a backyard flock.

- Most poultry raisers get their start with day-old chicks, usually through mail order.

- The four principles of successful brooding are heat, water, feed, and sanitation.

- Many people who raise exhibition poultry are eager to help beginners get a good start.

Chapter 4

A Home to Roost In

In This Chapter

- ◆ Chickens aren't very picky about their coops
- ◆ The meanings of "free range"
- ◆ Designing and building your coop
- ◆ A word about fencing

You've heard me say (and you'll hear it again) that raising chickens is simple: it's humans who make it complicated. Nowhere is this more evident than in housing. If you were surprised to see how many different kinds of chickens there are, wait until you see where they live!

When Everybody Had Chickens

When I was a boy (in the 1940s), our Rhode Island Reds lived in a corner of the garage, sectioned off with a chicken wire wall. My dad cut a chicken-size door, sometimes called a pop hole, leading to an outside run. The whole setup couldn't have cost more than a few dollars.

Since then I have lived on three different farms. Each one had an old-fashioned chicken coop in place, because not long ago nearly all farms raised chickens, along with cows, horses, and pigs. By "old-fashioned," I mean a simple slope-roofed shed about 10' × 20', with a chicken door and a people door, and windows on the south wall. None of them probably ever housed more than 50 chickens, and most likely none had been used since the rise of egg-and-broiler factories put small home flocks out of business in the mid-1900s. (The horses and pigs went next, and now many farms don't even have cows, but the decline in small family farms and the rise of agribusiness started with chickens.)

We've raised chickens in these old coops, we've had chickens just running loose in the barn, and we've made and used several styles of houses custom-built for small flocks as demonstration models for magazine articles. The chickens had no preferences. Their first concern every morning was to get outside! Most chicken coops are designed for people, not chickens.

What About Free-Range?

Before deciding what kind of chicken house to build, you'll want to consider some very basic details, such as how much space you can allot to your birds. Most small flock owners are interested in free-range chickens, partly because they are opposed to medicated, cage-raised birds. It's also much more fun to watch a bird scratching in the dirt than one sitting in a cage. But what is free-range all about, anyway?

Talk about free range! This chicken couldn't possibly use all of that space, and in fact, lives in a cage in the house. But isn't it a nice picture?

(Photo: Ondra Craw, Chelan, Washington)

It doesn't necessarily mean the chicken has the whole world to roam in. From a practical standpoint, the essential element is access to clean soil, with its various life forms ranging from worms to grass to grasshoppers, along with sunshine, fresh air, and exercise. This setup doesn't require acres per bird. In fact, to get chicks started on learning to forage at an early age, or simply to keep them occupied, some people put small clumps of sod in the brooder. Sod can entertain and benefit older confined birds as well, but there are many other options. In other words, between the extremes of the layer in the cage and the jungle fowl in the tree are many gradations of "free-range."

At the top of the scale would be the totally free chicken, allowed to wander anywhere, which usually isn't very far. Ours have always been content to remain somewhere between the henhouse and the people house, which is less than 50 yards.

Next would be a perimeter fence, which we have considered, to keep them off the patio and the porch, and out of the flowerbeds. Fencing is a topic in itself: we'll look at that later in this chapter. The point here is that one way to raise free-range chickens is with a coop inside a fenced-in area.

Moveable Pens

The so-called "chicken tractor" is a pen that can be moved to a fresh location daily, or as required. The house (coop) and yard (or run) are combined in one unit. The chicken isn't actually "free," in the sense that it can roam at will, but it does have daily access to fresh grass and clean ground, as well as fresh air and sunshine. Although this system can be used with fairly large flocks and large tracts of land, it's especially attractive for a flock of three or four and a relatively small backyard.

Garden Pens

Similar small moveable or temporary pens can also be used to good advantage in gardens. As crops are harvested, the chickens get to glean the leftovers and whatever else they can find, while adding fertilizer and stirring everything together with their endless scratching.

Garden pens need be nothing more than cages, if you carry the birds to them from their henhouse every day. For example, if you have 4' × 8' raised garden beds, a simple 4' × 8' frame covered with chicken wire could easily be moved from bed to bed, as needed. Of course, be sure to provide water and shade. Some creative people with large gardens have made the pens a permanent feature, rotating the chickens and crops as necessary. The same idea can be applied to greenhouses, where chickens provide the added benefit of body heat.

If you live on a small lot in town, your options might be somewhat limited: you're probably looking at a small structure in a permanent location with a rather restricted run. This doesn't mean you can't "exercise the chickens" the way you exercise the dog (without the Frisbee, of course). Just leave them out of the pen for a while every day, while you watch their chicken antics. Obviously they must be tame enough to be easy to catch when it's time for them to go back in the pen, but for most people and chickens, that's no problem.

Designing a Chicken Coop

The biggest innovations in chicken raising in the past few years have involved coop design. Not long ago, a chicken coop was a shed, pure and simple, with an occasional A-frame, and most held at least 50 or 100 chickens. Today you're limited only by your imagination, or in some cases, your budget. Coops for two to three birds are commonplace.

How do you start? Plan on 3 to 4 square feet per bird. A coop needs a door for the birds, and a door or some kind of access for you to gather eggs and do the housecleaning. But it doesn't have to be big enough for you to stand up in, or even enter, like the old coops were. If you can do what needs to be done simply by reaching in from outside, that's fine.

Coops need a window for light and ventilation. The birds need roosts, and a place to lay eggs (a nest box); several hens will share one nest. The coop obviously needs a roof and four walls, to protect the birds from weather and predators. Floors can be impervious, such as concrete, which is easy to clean and can deter some predators; or earthen, which is absorbent, warmer, and cheaper. Wooden floors are not recommended for permanent coops because of both cleaning and rodent concerns.

Roofs must obviously be waterproof and in cold climates can be insulated. Commercial insulation tends to absorb moisture, which can be a serious problem in a chicken house because chicken manure is so moist, and wet insulation doesn't insulate. A vapor barrier is essential. Chickens will peck at foam-type insulation, so that needs to be covered. In most cases a double wall, the dead air space providing the insulation, will suffice.

Last but not least, a poultry shelter should be pleasant and attractive, especially if it will be visible to neighbors. But you don't want to look at a shanty either. Most homesteader types can accomplish all this with materials that are either on hand or can be scrounged, and almost everyone has budget constrictions.

This budget coop made good use of recycled materials.

(Photo: Steve Belanger, Columbus, Wisconsin)

The Design Process

Put all of this into your brain, shake it up, and see what comes out. The options are endless, and putting it all together can be fun. It will challenge your creativity. If you have cabinet-making skills and the tools to go with them, you might choose a more elaborate design than someone who has never sawed a board or driven a nail. If you have a talent for design, you can probably sit down and dash off half a dozen sketches in less time than it will take somebody else to search books and the Internet for the detailed, step-by-step instructions they need even to construct a basic four-walls-and-a-roof coop. And if you have money, you can spend a lot of it on various ready-made chicken coops or by hiring professionals to do the work.

Cocktail Conversation

Ready-made coops are available in many styles and sizes, with names that would surely puzzle old-time chicken raisers! There is the "Egg-Cart'n" chicken tractor, the "eglu," "Chick-N-Pen" (also "Barn and Hutch"), "Octa-Coop," and the "HenSpa." For some people, ready-made coops are very good solutions to the problem of housing chickens in an urban or suburban environment. For others, they might provide a spark of inspiration.

This explains why there are literally hundreds, maybe thousands, of different plans for chicken coops. The best we can do here is to offer some general suggestions from the standpoint of the chicken and the convenience of the caretaker.

Can a chicken house look like a playhouse? Why not? Use your imagination and have fun!

(Photo: Mary Jane Hawkins, Bland, Missouri)

Three Coop Categories

The small-flock owner today has three basic coop categories to choose from.

♦ First, the very simple, often temporary (for summer use only) shelter that is basically just a place to lay eggs and sleep, or to get out of the rain or hot sun

♦ Second, the "standard" chicken house, a solid structure in a permanent location

♦ Third, the moveable coop

All three involve similar, and dissimilar, design considerations.

The minimalist is the simple A-frame structure that is easily built and moved. Space requirements are minimal because feed and water are provided outside. A-frames are commonly associated with summer pasture, but they provide economical housing year-round in milder climates, and can be used anywhere with protection against wind and snow.

This is a simple, basic A-frame shelter.

(Photo: J. D. Belanger)

Then there is the standard chicken house, which is anything but standard nowadays. It can look like an old-fashioned chicken coop downsized, a chicken cottage or doll house, or it can be a small replica of the owner's architect-designed copper-roofed mansion, sort of a Taj MahCoop. It's a permanent structure and an architectural feature. There are fieldstone chicken coops and no doubt a few made of brick. They can be plain or fancy, businesslike or whimsical.

Among the advantages of the standard coop: it can be pleasantly landscaped to disguise, soften, and shade the structure; and it can be made accessible to water and electricity, the latter being important for winter egg production. It requires more cleaning than a moveable facility, but on the other hand, it enables you to recycle nutrients through the compost bin for use when and where they're most needed. Being permanent, it can also be constructed of heavier, more durable materials, which can be important for protection from the elements and predators. Also because of its permanency, it requires thinking about such things as location of the compost bin and garden, shade, prevailing winds, proximity to water, and ease of feeding, including getting 50-pound bags of feed to the house, if it's large enough to include feed storage.

In practice, many backyard coops today are no larger than a doghouse, and the feed is stored in the garage or garden shed.

Third is the moveable pen, which has become very popular and which some people now call a "chicken tractor." These obviously are limited in size and weight because they're meant to be moved on a daily basis. If the pen is 8 feet long, you move it 8 feet a day. The chickens get fresh grass and a clean place, the lawn gets mowed and fertilized without being destroyed, and you get maybe two minutes of exercise.

With a little paint and a few flowers, a poultry pen can make a positive statement in a landscape.

(Photo: J. D. Belanger)

The coop shown in this figure was designed and built by my son Steve, and when he moved, I inherited it. That brought my total to five, but this was my favorite. Later I left it in one place, landscaped it, and kept guineas in it. It's 6 feet long, wide and high, with the 2' × 6' henhouse providing additional space 3 feet off the ground. The framework is made of 2 × 2s, the exterior is 1" × 8" boxcar siding, and it required 15 feet of 5-foot-high chicken wire and 10 feet of 3-foot chicken wire. The roof is fiberglass and very lightweight, although I think the hens would prefer a darker interior. Also, there are four nests inside, but six hens always share the lower two. It would be easy to make another door so eggs could be collected from outside, but it works just fine the way it is. There are two roosts inside, and birds also roost on the 2 × 2 "handles" that are used to move it. The bottom is secured with treated 1 × 8 boards to discourage varmints. The large (wire) door on the front provides access for feeding and watering, and the smaller (wood) door on the house part makes it easy to gather eggs and clean the coop.

Look at pictures of coops (there are entire books on the topic, and more on the web), and you'll probably get some ideas of your own. If you have no building skills or experience, you no doubt can find a friend, neighbor, relative, or co-worker who would be happy to give you a hand, and even furnish the tools—especially if you offer to barter for some fresh eggs when the project is completed! If all else fails, a growing number of companies now provide coop kits, which are easily assembled by the average person who is somewhat handy with tools. Some companies even provide fully assembled coops (see Appendix B).

Fencing

Chickens are easy to confine. They don't lean against or climb on fences like goats do, and they don't root under them like pigs. Most of the heavier breeds of chickens aren't much inclined to fly, and will be kept in their place with a mere 2- or 3-foot-high barrier. Higher fences might be needed for some, such as Leghorns and bantams, or you can clip the feathers on one wing—one only—to prevent flying.

In many cases the fence is needed not so much to keep the chickens in, but to keep predators out. It's not uncommon for the family canine pet, who "wouldn't think of harming a chicken," to suddenly become a killer. Neighbors' dogs are even worse. The greatest danger from any predator (except hawks) comes at night, so securing the flock inside a tight building at dusk is the best insurance. If hawks are a big problem you might have to consider a pen with a roof. Lightweight bird netting, such as is used to protect fruit trees, should suffice for that.

Fencing can take the form of poultry netting or mesh. Poultry netting (sometimes called chicken wire) comes in various forms and weights, with hexagonal holes. It's available in 20-, 14-, and 12-gauge wire, with 1- or 2-inch holes, from 2 feet to 4 feet in height, in rolls of any length. There are also plastic-coated versions. Chicken wire is commonly attached to wood fence posts with fencing staples, although it can also be wired to metal T-posts, which are usually more convenient, and unless you cut your own posts, cheaper.

For larger flocks in more spacious settings, the ideal fencing is the more expensive (naturally) electrified poultry netting, which also comes in various configurations but is

Cacklings

Wing clipping involves cutting off the flight feathers (the 10 large feathers) on one wing only (which throws the bird off balance). Do not cut into the hollow portion of the quill. The feathers will grow back after the next molt.

commonly 42 inches high. This type of fence is portable, easily moved, and can be electrified with either plug-in or solar-powered fence chargers. If predators are a serious problem for you, this is the one to consider. Learn more at www.premier1supplies. com/fencing.php?species_id=6.

The Least You Need to Know

- ◆ Most chicken coops are designed for the convenience, and the tastes, of the caretaker.

- ◆ The benefits of "free-range" can be had even in limited spaces.

- ◆ Chickens need about 3 to 4 square feet of coop space, plus an outdoor area.

- ◆ A variety of ready-made chicken coops are now available, if you have more money than time and skill.

Chapter 5

The Amazing Egg

In This Chapter

- ◆ Where eggs come from
- ◆ Egg quality, inside and out
- ◆ The role of the rooster
- ◆ The broody hen

The egg is nature's perfect package, as well as nature's most perfect food. In terms of protein, it's the standard against which all other foods are measured.

It has been a symbol of rebirth—of Earth since ancient times, and of humankind in the current era. It has been used as medicine and in magic potions, heralded in song and story, and decorated by delighted children and by renowned goldsmiths for delighted czarinas.

There is much more to an egg than meets the eye—or the frying pan.

How Eggs Are Made

Most people don't see eggs until they reach the dairy case in the supermarket. Sure, they know chickens layed them, but they're not familiar with the process. You, of course, as a chicken farmer, know very well where that egg on your plate came from, but you should also be aware that there's much, much more to know about the egg. Astound your friends and relatives with some of these interesting facts, and they'll be amazed at how smart you got since you started raising chickens.

Which Came First?

The next time somebody brings up the old puzzle about the chicken and egg, you might casually mention that a hen's body already contains every egg she will ever lay, and then some, before she even hatches out of her own shell: all 4,000 or so!

These are, of course, *ova* (singular *ovum*), the Latin word for egg. Eggs come from ovaries, which are present in plants and female vertebrates, including humans and chickens. In other words, chickens have no monopoly on eggs; they're everywhere. Technically, even peaches and apples are eggs.

Most females are born with two ovaries, but in the chicken, the right one atrophies and becomes useless. The functioning ovary is located on the left of the backbone, midway between the neck and the tail.

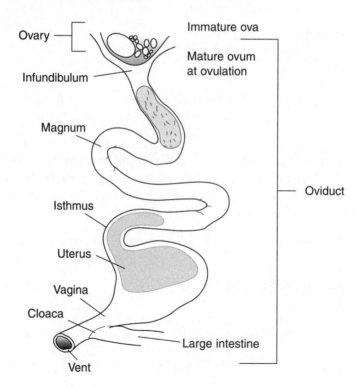

The Developing Egg

When a pullet matures, usually at 18 to 22 weeks, so do the ova, one by one. As an ovum acquires layers of yolk, it's released into the first section of the oviduct, the infundibulum (see diagram). This is where it's fertilized, if a rooster was present and active anytime within the past 7 to 10 days. (A rooster doesn't have to perform every day to have fertile eggs, although most do their best to try.) Whether it's fertilized or not, the yolk passes through the albumen-secreting section of the oviduct, the magnum, and then into the isthmus, where the shell membranes are added. The yolk then moves to the uterus, or shell gland, where fluid is added, and the shell is formed. The entire process takes 24 to 26 hours.

An hour or so after an egg is layed, the process starts all over again. There are always eggs at various stages of development in the works.

Egg Production

Although human females ovulate approximately once a month (and just like hens, with or without a male), chickens ovulate almost every day, with some exceptions. But don't expect a hen to produce 365 eggs a year! Around 180 is considered average. For some breeds, even that would be a lot. Egg production can be affected by several factors, including seasonal light, the molting process, broodiness, and stress.

Egg production is related to the function of the anterior pituitary gland and its production of luteinizing hormones, all of which is affected by light. For this reason, most hens start to lay fewer eggs as the days grow shorter in fall. Although this is in large part a factor of heredity (breed, variety, and strain), the hen can be stimulated by artificial light. The ideal is 14 hours a day, which is easily achieved with a timer. A rule of thumb for light intensity is that you should be able to read a newspaper at hen level, or one 40-watt bulb for each 100 square feet of space. Some people advise against fluorescent lights on the grounds that their cycling has a "disco" effect that upsets chickens. Others simply warn that a "warm" wavelength fluorescent bulb is required, since the more common "cool" bulb does not stimulate the hen. In addition, fluorescent bulbs can't be used with dimmer switches, which can otherwise be used to regulate light intensity. Limited research suggests that the new CF bulbs should work as well as incandescent bulbs.

The discovery of the effects of light on egg production was one of the factors in the development of huge egg factories. If you don't provide artificial light in winter, it won't hurt the hens; in fact, it's natural. But you'll get fewer eggs.

Shorter days also cause chickens to molt, or lose their old feathers and grow new ones in preparation for cold weather. Since molting is a gradual process—they don't shed all their feathers at once—it can cover a span of three or four months. Egg production suffers as nutrients are channeled into feather growth, but this varies with the breed.

Fox Alert _____

If your chickens have been laying so well that you have been selling the extra eggs, rest assured that just at the time you have a nice little side business going, production will plummet, for any or all of the reasons mentioned. Don't count your chickens before they're hatched, or your eggs before they're layed.

Some birds not bred for high egg production, and therefore not great layers anyway, might stop altogether for a month, or even two, whereas commercial strains of laying breeds might not quit at all.

Those commercial layers aren't as likely to go broody either, since broodiness has been bred out of them. Hens that go broody, meaning they want to sit on eggs and hatch them instead of laying more, can result in backyarders eating oatmeal instead of eggs. And yes, a hen can go broody without a rooster, too.

Egg production can decline for many other reasons, including stress caused by predators, dogs, children, or weather.

Structure of the Egg

It's obvious that an egg is not merely an elliptical shell containing a yolk and a white. In addition to being a link in the continuation of life (if it's fertilized) and therefore a miracle, it's an astoundingly complex organism, despite its simple appearance. Several features are of special interest and importance, if only because sooner or later someone is going to ask you about them, and as a chicken raiser, you must be an expert!

One very common question and misconception concerns that whitish cordlike mass found attached to the yolk. No, it has nothing to do with the rooster. It's called the *chalazae* (ka-LAY-zee). It's nothing but twisted strands of protein, or egg white, which centers the yolk in the shell. Some cooks go to a lot of trouble to remove it, but that's a waste of time. It's a sign of a fresh egg and gradually unwinds with age.

Another sign of freshness is the air cell found at the blunt end of the egg. It doesn't exist in a freshly layed egg: the entire shell is filled. The air space starts to develop at once and increases with age. This explains why you can test the freshness of an egg by placing it in water. Fresh eggs sink; old eggs float because the air space has increased; and in-between eggs just sort of hang there (blunt side up), depending on their age. Store eggs with the pointy end down and the air cell won't force the yolk to be off-center.

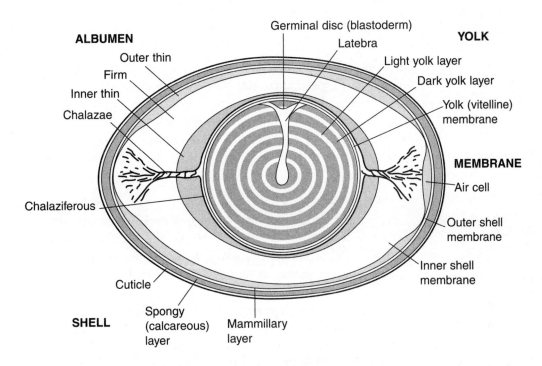

ALBUMEN
- Outer thin
- Firm
- Inner thin
- Chalazae

Germinal disc (blastoderm)
Latebra

YOLK
- Light yolk layer
- Dark yolk layer
- Yolk (vitelline) membrane

Chalaziferous

MEMBRANE
- Air cell
- Outer shell membrane
- Inner shell membrane

Cuticle

SHELL
- Spongy (calcareous) layer
- Mammillary layer

Notice the germinal disc, or *blastodisk*. This is present in all eggs, but if fertilization takes place this is where it happens, before the shell is formed. It then becomes a *blastoderm*. If a fertilized egg is refrigerated, as eating eggs should be, there will be no embryonic development. If the fertile egg is kept in a warm environment, the chick will start to grow at the blastoderm.

Another item of interest and importance is the *bloom*. This is a moist outer membrane that coats a freshly layed egg, and the reason a just-layed egg appears wet. It dries quickly, forming a barrier that keeps moisture in and bacteria out. It's important to know, because washing an egg removes the bloom. Avoid washing eggs whenever possible, in favor of brushing or scraping off any dirt. If an egg must be washed and the bloom destroyed, don't plan on it keeping too long or hatching.

def•i•ni•tion

The twisted strands of egg white that center the yolk in the shell are the **chalazae**. The **blastodisc** is the site on the yolk where fertilization takes place. A fertilized blastodisc is called a **blastoderm**—the very beginning of the new chick. The **bloom** is the natural coating of a fresh egg that helps keep it fresh.

Eggs and Blood

On occasion you might find eggs with blood spots on the shell, usually caused by a small rupture as the egg is layed by an immature pullet. This might also be caused by the northern fowl mite. It irritates hens' vents, causing a scab to form. When the vent is stretched in egg laying, the scab breaks and blood streaks the egg. Coccidiosis, a disease caused by internal parasites, causes intestinal bleeding, which can also result in bloody eggs. (See Chapter 8 for more on this topic.) Spots on the shell have no effect on the eating quality of the egg.

Blood spots in the egg itself, inside the shell, are considered normal in 1 to 3 percent of the eggs produced and are of no concern to either the chicken or the consumer. Like the chalazae, these spots are sometimes seen as evidence of a growing chick, but again, there's no connection. A blood spot occurs when the capillaries fail to seal off completely during ovulation, releasing a bit of blood into the egg. You can remove the spot if you want to, but the egg is edible either way. Since most city people today don't know that and find the spots unappetizing, eggs to be sold are *candled*, or inspected. Eggs with spots are used for baking and other manufacturing purposes.

def·i·ni·tion

Candling refers to examining the inside of an egg by looking through it, with the aid of a bright light source (originally, a candle) on the far side, in a darkened room. Commercially, eggs are candled to eliminate those with blood spots. In hatching eggs, developing embryos can be seen and infertile eggs disposed of.

Double yolks result when two ova mature at the same time. It's most frequent in pullet eggs. Much rarer is an egg within an egg, caused when a formed egg is forced back through the oviduct. Both are edible conversation pieces.

Eggshell Colors and Abnormalities

Many backyarders want brown eggs, or blue or green, if only for the novelty. Shell color is largely a function of breed, but even if you have a breed that lays brown or blue eggs, the color can vary.

Color Genetics

All chicken eggs start out white. Pigments called porphyrins are deposited while the egg is still being formed. Brown eggs from breeds such as the Rhode Island Red derive the brown pigment protoporphryn from hemoglobin in the blood. Eggs from

Araucanas have a blue pigment called oocyanin, a product of bile formation. Various crosses have resulted in a wide range of shell colors, even though blue is dominant. For example, cross a blue layer with another blue layer, or a blue layer with one that lays white eggs, and you'll get a hen that lays blue eggs. However, cross a blue egg layer with a light brown layer, and you'll get green eggs, while blue × dark brown = olive brown.

> **Cocktail Conversation**
>
> "Eggshell white" might describe a paint color, but it certainly doesn't describe a chicken egg. In 1926, a researcher named Kope isolated 13 shades of brown eggs. In 1933, the gene for blue eggs was identified as dominant by a Professor Punnett.

There are obviously many other possibilities from the crosses, as well as the 13 shades of brown. French Marans and Welsummers are noted for their dark brown, often rich mahogany or chocolate-colored eggs. Fourteen genes are responsible for brown eggs, and they aren't well understood, but some breeders have reported that when selecting for dark brown shells, they get fewer eggs. (Genetically, egg quality is passed on by the male.) This gives rise to the theory that the shells are dark because they pass through the oviduct more slowly, thus accruing more pigment.

However, even with these breeds shell color varies with the bird, the feed, the season, and other factors. Older hens often lay eggs with paler shells, and color intensity is also affected by heat, stress, viral infections, and other factors. Most home flocks don't produce eggs of uniform color, but the variety makes them more interesting.

Brown eggs are preferred in some localities, white in others. Some people like the novelty of blue or green eggs. Some small egg producers have wowed the folks at farmers' markets by selling cartons of eggs of many colors, including pinkish and speckled, which certainly sets them apart. (And reportedly, some people think brown eggs come from free-range birds, while white ones come from caged layers.)

Some people think brown eggs have better flavor than white ones, but that's subjective. The bottom line is, there is no scientific or nutritional difference between an egg of one color and an egg of any other color.

> **Cacklings**
>
> If you find a brown egg before the bloom dries, you can rub off the brown color. Once dried, nothing will remove it. Some children (of any age) think this is neat.

Abnormal Shells

If you raise chickens for eggs, sooner or later you'll find eggs with unusual shells. Abnormalities can include wrinkled shells, misshapen eggs, reduced shell thickness, and even shell-less eggs. A lot can happen to an egg on that short trip from the ovary to the nest, and abnormal shells aren't really uncommon, so don't get all excited and think you'll sell one on eBay. Eggs can also be perfectly round, very oblong, or some really weird shape, but considering that they are very plastic before they have a hard shell, these shapes are understandable. Sometimes defects can be attributed to diet, but in general, they're to be expected once in a while.

Linda C. Knepp found several eggs with abnormal shells like this one from her young hens. Shell defects aren't uncommon enough to call the newspaper, like some people do.

(Photo: Linda C. Knepp, North Platte, Nebraska)

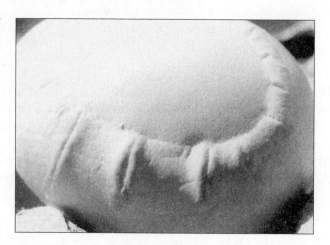

Laying and Collecting

To a chicken, an egg has nothing to do with your breakfast, cake, or custard. A hen lays an egg to perpetuate her species, not to feed you. That's why the natural time for egg-laying is in spring, when the day length is increasing. This timing makes it more likely that the eggs will hatch when the weather is warm and food will be plentiful. There are stories of barnyard bantams being hatched in a November snowstorm and surviving the winter, but in general, egg production shuts down as the days grow shorter, unless humans interfere with artificial light (and selective breeding) for their own interests.

Cocktail Conversation

Until just a few generations ago, eggs were plentiful and cheap in spring and summer, but scarce and expensive in fall and winter. This changed when science discovered the connection between light and ovulation, the importance of vitamin D for normal calcium absorption and utilization, and other factors affecting egg production. Farmers started using these discoveries in their henhouses, and eggs became an inexpensive, everyday food.

We have seen why most hens lay an egg every 25 hours on average. This means they lay an hour later each day, which explains why sometimes you find eggs in the morning and sometimes in the afternoon. However, the system shuts down at night, so an egg that's ready to be layed at dusk will be held over until morning—which also explains why most eggs are layed in the morning. With just a few hens, you'll know when to expect to find eggs. With a larger flock, eggs should be gathered three or four times a day for maximum cleanliness and freshness.

Eggs are layed in clutches. That is, a hen lays as many eggs as she can cover or sit on, usually 12 to 18 or so. She then sets, or goes broody. (Remember that not all breeds go broody, and many have had the trait bred out of them.) When this happens she quits laying, due to a hormone (prolactin) released by the pituitary, the same gland connected with light exposure and laying.

Fox Alert

Do be careful when gathering eggs while there's a hen on the nest. If she's in the process of laying an egg and you disrupt her, the egg could break while still inside her body, with serious consequences.

If you put all your eggs in one basket, be sure to watch that basket!

(Photo: Gale Miko, New Jersey)

Ordinarily, a hen lays an egg and leaves the nest. However, if she's thinking of going broody, she stays on the nest, even when you want to gather the eggs. Depending on how serious she is, she might fluff up in a huff or peck at your hand and snap a wing at you. This can upset children and timid people, but these are just signs of impending broodiness. Such hens are seldom life-threatening, and often calm down when you slowly and gently reach under them for the egg or eggs. In most cases she soon rejoins the flock and forgets about motherhood.

The Rooster

A hen will lay eggs without a rooster, but the eggs won't hatch. Most small flock owners, those folks this book is written for, won't have a rooster. But yours might be the exception, and every chicken raiser should be aware of the basic facts of life anyway.

There should be 1 rooster for 20 hens in the light or egg-type breeds, such as the 4.5-pound Leghorn; and 1 for 10 to 12 in the heavy breeds, such as the 9-pound Brahma. Older roosters (two to four years old) often don't pursue mating with as much vigor or accuracy, so the male/female ratio should be increased.

As with the hen, the rooster requires a certain amount of light for reproduction. The hormone level of the rooster's blood must reach a certain level before the sperm grows and matures.

The rooster indicates his interest by courting behavior, which can include a kind of strutting dance and an impressive display of wings and feathers. Often the hen leads the male on a merry chase. If she is receptive, she crouches. The male steps on her back, grasping her neck feathers by his beak, and squats, so the vents touch, and releases the semen.

When birds mate there is no penetration. The rooster's small sex organ merely touches the hen's organ, which she exposes at the moment of mating. And a moment is all it takes. The rooster steps off and probably crows, the hen fluffs her feathers, and they go about their business.

Some breeds, because of their dimensions or feathering, have difficulty mating. Cornish, very large fowl, and some bantams have short, heavy legs, extreme muscle development, or wide bodies that interfere with breeding. Profuse feathering also poses problems: many Cochin breeders clip some of the vent feathers before breeding season.

The sperm congregates in "nests" in folded recesses of the oviduct, where it can remain viable for as long as three or four weeks, although fertility declines considerably after the first week. Older hens stay fertile longer than younger ones, but neither requires the daily attentions of a rooster in order to lay fertile eggs. As a sperm leaves the "nest," it moves up the funnel of infundibulum, where fertilization occurs if an ovum is released from the ovary.

Handling Eggs

After a fertilized egg has been layed, it must be handled properly in order to protect its hatchability. In nature the hen selects a cool, dark place for a nest, hopefully where egg-loving animals such as skunks and opossums won't find it. Whether we humans hatch eggs in an incubator or put them back under a broody hen later, gathering them daily helps protect them from those predators; gathering keeps them cleaner and prevents them from accidentally getting broken; and we can control the optimum temperature and humidity to enhance hatchability.

Ideally, eggs should be gathered several times a day and stored at a temperature of between 50°F to 65°F with a relative humidity of 75 percent. A cool basement is perfect. In dry conditions, place the eggs in covered boxes lined with 3 to 6 inches of clean bedding that has been slightly dampened.

Although eggs can remain viable for longer periods under optimal conditions, it's best not to store them for more than 14 days, and 7 is better. Turn them daily to prevent the yolk from floating to the surface of the white and adhering to the shell's inner surface.

Incubation

I presented an overview of the basics of incubation and mechanical incubators in reference to getting started with chickens in Chapter 3. Here are a few additional helpful ideas in more detail with emphasis on the broody hen.

Like most bantams, this Black Japanese is an excellent setting hen and mother.

(Photo: Larry and Koralyn Kibbee, Manhattan, Montana)

A hen lays a clutch of eggs, normally 12 to 18, before starting to set. The first ones layed don't begin to develop until she starts setting, so all of the chicks hatch within hours of each other even if the eggs are layed days apart. When we humans hatch eggs we usually want enough to put under a hen or to fill an incubator. (Don't add new eggs to those already started in an incubator.)

You cannot force a hen to set, nor do you know if you're going to have a broody hen when you want to set the eggs. You can tell a hen is going broody when she stays on the nest for an inordinately long time and tries to fight you off if you delicately slip your hand under her to search for eggs.

In general, the Continental and Mediterranean breeds cannot be expected to go broody. This is especially true of the highly refined cage layer varieties of Leghorns, which would become extinct if it weren't for humans. The Asiatic breeds are usually excellent broodies and mothers. Bantams—especially Cochins and Silkies—are often used to hatch eggs of larger birds because they're so good at it. American and English breeds are okay, but variable, and some hens will hatch eggs but largely ignore the chicks when they hatch, including Cornish and Old English Games.

On a self-sufficient homestead or subsistence farm, letting a hen go broody might make sense. It can also be a lot of fun on a hobby farm: nothing is quite as pastoral as a hen scratching in the dooryard, surrounded by her scurrying chicks, nor as endearing as bright-eyed chicks peeping out from beneath their mother's fluffy breast feathers. One hurdle for the city or suburban poultry raiser might be the lack of a rooster, which obviously is essential for such an endeavor.

But there are other hurdles as well, such as predators of all shapes and sizes, including the chicks' own "aunts," who sometimes seem incapable of distinguishing between a fuzzy chick and a mouse. Ideally, a broody hen is confined to her own pen, away from the rest of the flock, and well fortified against everything from snakes and rats to raccoons and coyotes, as well as weather extremes—and lice and mites. Hatching eggs is fraught with dangers!

When a hen goes broody and you intend to use her for setting, add cracked corn to her feed to help develop a warm brood pouch on her breast. Move her to a secluded nest and give her a couple of dummy eggs to sit on for two days. Powder her with an approved insecticide: lice and mites in sufficient numbers can kill a setting hen. (In the good old days we used tobacco stems, which were available at our local feed dealer, for both chicken and pigeon nests. Today, Sevin® is easier to find.)

If the hen decides motherhood isn't for her after all and leaves the nest, no eggs were risked. If she's still sitting tight after two days, she'll probably last for the whole 21 required for hatching. So warm the stored eggs to room temperature and place them in the nest, removing the dummies. Use only as many eggs as the hen can cover, often 10 to 12. If any stick out and she tries to tuck them back in, another one will stick out, and very likely several of them won't hatch.

A setting hen probably leaves the nest once a day for food, water, and exercise. She turns the eggs, as needed, and in many cases will nudge a bad egg out of the nest entirely. Other than that she'll be nearly comatose, in a state of partial hibernation. Her temperature drops, and her metabolic processes slow. Any immature yolks inside her body are resorbed; she won't lay more eggs while broody. This, of course, is why people who sell eggs don't want hens that go broody.

> **Cocktail Conversation**
>
> A bantam hen can cover as many as 24 bantam eggs, or 8 to 10 eggs of a large breed. She won't know the difference and will be an equally good mother in either case.

On or about the seventh day, you should candle the eggs. This procedure can be as simple as holding a bright flashlight behind the egg in a darkened room, allowing you to see through the translucent shell. For somewhat better results, place a bright light in an enclosed box with one hole, slightly smaller than an egg. Hold the egg up to the hole to examine the contents.

If you see a reddish, spiderlike body in it, the egg is fertile and the embryo is on schedule. A black loop is a blood ring, which indicates that the embryo started to develop, and then died. If you see nothing, it might mean you were one of the kids in biology class who could never see anything through the microscope, or the egg was not fertilized. You might want to leave it for a few days and check again, but it's best to remove and dispose of any eggs not showing normal embryonic development. You have heard about "rotten eggs" even if you've never encountered one, and you probably don't want to. In a worst-case scenario an egg can explode in the nest, causing all kinds of yucky problems.

Chicken eggs normally hatch in 21 days. And within hours, the hen and her brood will be out and about, adding immeasurable charm to your chicken farm of any size.

The Least You Need to Know

- A hen lays an egg every 25 hours or so—therefore, a little later every day.

- There is no nutritional difference between white and brown (or blue-green) eggs.

- It takes about 21 days for a chicken egg to hatch.

- Not all hens want to sit on nests to hatch eggs.

Chapter 6

Chicken Growth and Development

In This Chapter

- How the egg came first
- A history of the chicken
- Chicken biology
- Fanciful feather facts

The answer to the classic chicken-and-egg question will shock many people, and it definitely sets birds apart from the animals we might be more familiar with. But then, there are many fascinating facts about chickens most people aren't aware of. The crass, commercial chicken raiser has no need to know many of them, but for anyone who raises chickens for pleasure, they make the birds all the more interesting.

First There Was an Egg

When you see a chicken's skeleton, such as the one shown in the following figure, what's your first reaction? If you're like most people, it's probably something like, "By golly, that sure looks like a dinosaur."

Looking at a chicken's skeleton, it's easy to believe that they're descended from dinosaurs.

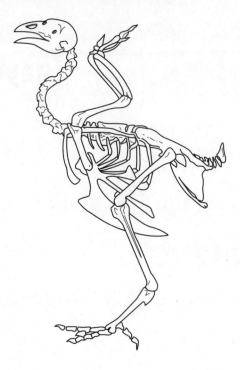

Scientists tell us that could be because birds evolved from dinosaurs. So at some point back in the Jurassic era, a dinosaur egg hatched that was maybe not quite what we'd call a bird, but not your normal everyday dinosaur, either. Eventually reptilian scales became feathers (some dinosaurs were feathered, and chickens still retain scaly feet and legs) and the first true bird was hatched.

So the answer to the old conundrum is clear: the egg came long before the chicken, but it didn't contain anything that would pass for a chicken today. Eventually it did, but it was a long, slow process.

Scientists say it's not likely that dinosaurs could be recreated from a mosquito encased in amber, as in *Jurassic Park*. However, some think they could reconstruct a dinosaur using chicken genes. Jack Horner, curator at the Museum of the Rockies and the first to uncover dinosaur eggs in the Western Hemisphere, is working on switching chicken genes on and off to bring back the ancestral traits—a dino-chicken. The museum, widely known for its collection of dinosaurs, has a laboratory devoted to the study of cellular and molecular paleontology.

Cocktail Conversation

You don't have to wait for the 50 to 100 years it's expected to take before the first dino-chicken appears. *Make Your Own Dinosaur Out of Chicken Bones* (Harper Paperbacks, 1997) is a fun book showing how to make an *Apatosaurus* skeleton from the bones of three chickens and a few household items. Written by Chris McGowan, a curator at the Royal Ontario Museum, this project neatly demonstrates the theory that birds evolved from dinosaurs, as well as teaching skeletal anatomy along with bird and dinosaur facts. As an added bonus, the book includes recipes for chicken soup and salad, so nothing goes to waste.

The first true chickens (*Gallus gallus*) were scratching and crowing in the jungles of southern Asia at least 8,000 years ago. Archeological evidence proves human interaction with chickens as far back as 7,400 years ago in China and Thailand. Chickens spread from the Harappan culture in the Indus Valley to Africa, Europe, and the rest of the world—including the Americas—long before Columbus. In fact, the discovery that chickens existed in South America a hundred years before Columbus landed gave weight to the theory that humans arrived in the Western Hemisphere via the Polynesian Islands, bringing their chickens with them.

The first European chickens came with Columbus on his second voyage, in 1493. The first colonists at Jamestown reportedly brought 500 chickens from home. Much later, many new breeds arrived in the Western Hemisphere after the opening of the Orient in the 1840s, creating a sensational "hen mania" in both Europe and America.

Cocktail Conversation

Chickens have played a large role in the study of history and archeology, but also in many other areas of research. Incubated eggs have long been used in classrooms to study embryology. But since chickens are easily bred and housed and mature rapidly, they have found many other uses as experimental animals. One recent example involves their role in the study of human ovarian cancer.

Even after they were found nearly everywhere that humans inhabit the planet, chickens continued to proliferate, as new varieties were developed and spread. The first edition of the American Poultry Association's *American Standard of Perfection* (1874) listed 41 breeds. There are now 60, and many varieties of each. Of course, hundreds of breeds are not officially recognized by the APA.

Biology of the Chicken

Some of the differences between birds and other animals are readily apparent: the feathers, beaks, wings, and so on. Some aren't visible or apparent: the hollow, light-weight bones that enable flight and the unique digestive system. Chickens differ from ordinary birds in some respects.

Combs

For example, only chickens have combs, those rubbery red ornamental appendages on their heads. Most people are aware, if only from cartoons, that roosters have larger combs than hens, but if you took a survey at the mall, how many shoppers could tell you that there are eight different types of combs, or what their purpose is?

Combs are a unique characteristic of chickens. This is a "single" comb, which is one of the eight types.

(Photo: Jill Peck, Brant, Michigan)

Combs help cool the birds. Chickens have no sweat glands. Blood circulating through the comb and wattles (those appendages dangling beneath the chin) cools much like water going through the radiator of a car. This then cools the car's engine, or in this case, the chicken's body.

Larger combs are obviously more useful in hot climates. Conversely, not only are they not as necessary in cool regions, but in very cold weather they can freeze. The

Chantecler chicken, bred in Canada to flourish in a northern climate, has a very small comb. The Leghorn and Ancona from Italy, and the Andalusian, Catalana, and Minorca from sunny Spain, all have large combs.

The types of combs are single, rose, pea, cushion, v-shaped, buttercup, strawberry, and silkie (or walnut). The males' combs are usually larger because combs are a secondary sexual characteristic. There is evidence that a chicken's comb size is related to dominance: those with large combs tend to be higher on the pecking order.

> **Cocktail Conversation**
>
> Most people know that roosters have larger combs than hens. Fewer are aware that some breeds have larger combs than others. This means a rooster of one breed might have a smaller comb than a hen of another breed.

A few other birds do have combs, or something similar, but the comb is the basis for identifying a chicken. The Latin word for comb is *gallus,* and the chicken is classified as *Gallus gallus* or *Gallus domesticus.*

Digestive System

"As scarce as hens' teeth" means pretty doggone rare, because chickens have none. Neither do they have what we would call a mouth, or at least a mouth with lips. In its place is the horny beak, which is part of the skull. Beaks are adapted to a bird's diet: meat-eating hawks and owls have curved beaks for tearing; seed-eating birds like grosbeaks have thick, powerful beaks for crushing; frog- and fish-eating herons and cranes have spearlike beaks; and ducks' beaks are more like spoons. The chicken is an omnivore, dining on both animal (including insects) and vegetable foods. It has what might be considered an all-purpose beak. Since food cannot be chewed, it must either be provided or pecked into a size that can be swallowed whole.

Fox Alert

Chickens can become crop bound (a condition also called sour crop), meaning there's an obstruction preventing food from leaving the crop and going into the gizzard. There are several possible causes, including ingesting pieces of plastic or other materials, and poor diet. If the crop becomes hard and distended, quick action is required, or the bird will die.

Force a tablespoon of sweet oil (olive or other cooking oil) down the bird's throat, followed by 2 tablespoons of warm water. Gently knead the crop, forcing the contents out of the mouth while holding the bird upside down. In extreme cases, surgery might be required.

The food first goes into the crop, a kind of sac or pouch on the front of the bird at the bottom of the neck, which is mainly for storage. You can usually feel material in the crop when you handle a bird.

From the crop, food passes to the gizzard. Gizzards should be familiar to anyone who has butchered a chicken or who has purchased a dressed chicken with the "giblets" (heart, gizzard, liver, and usually the neck) included. Pickled gizzards are also a popular snack food in some places. It's an oval organ, about the size of an egg, consisting of two very strong muscles with an extremely tough lining. Grit, or small pebbles or gravel, will usually be present (not in a dressed, store-bought chicken, hopefully). The gizzard and grit crush and grind food, thus serving the same purpose as teeth.

The food then passes to the small intestine, where it is digested and absorbed with the aid of enzymes. The residue is disposed of via the *cloaca*, a Latin word meaning "common sewer." The term is appropriate, considering that it's the channel for both waste and reproduction, and that waste consists of both urine and feces.

Actually, a chicken's urine is quite viscous—chickens don't have bladders—and it's voided at the same time as the intestinal contents. Urine is the white or cream-colored portion of the droppings. All-white deposits indicate only urine is being voided. This information should help understand the mess a few chickens can make on your patio or deck and outdoor furniture.

Skeletal System

Birds have pneumatic bones, making their bodies lighter for flight, and chickens have nine air sacs as part of their respiratory system, also making the body lighter.

Birds must be light enough to fly (even if they'd rather walk, like most chickens), but their skeletons must be strong enough to support their bodies and to protect their internal organs. This need has led to some important differences between mammalian and avian skeletons.

Fox Alert

Birds breathe not with a diaphragm, but by the movement of the sternum and rib cage. Holding a bird tightly so the breastbone can't move in and out can cause suffocation. This can be a problem when young children hold chicks.

In birds, some sections of the vertebrae are fused together, providing rigidity needed for flight. The sternum, or breastbone, provides a large surface for the attachment of the large breast muscles needed for flight. Avian ribs are different in that one rib is connected to the next by overlying flaps, adding strength to the rib cage so it won't collapse during flight. The tail bones are fused, in a short section.

Since a large head would make flying more difficult, a bird has a much smaller head, proportionate to its body, than other animals. However, most birds have long necks, serving several important functions. With such a rigid body, picking up food from the ground would be difficult without a long, flexible neck. That flexibility also acts as a shock absorber, protecting the delicate brain tissues during jarring landings. In addition, the neck allows the bird to alter its center of gravity when changing from the walking or perching upright position to the more horizontal position of flying.

The hollow bones do more than reduce weight. Some, called *pneumatic* bones, are actually part of the respiratory or breathing system. In case anyone asks, these bones include the skull, humerus, clavicle, sternum, pelvic girdle, lumbar, and sacral verte-brate.

Cocktail Conversation

The chicken's only significant gland of the skin is the uropygial gland, also called preen gland, oil gland, or oil bag, depending on whether you're a scientist, a poultry judge, or a worker in a poultry slaughtering plant. It's found near the tip of the tail (also called the uropygium, or variously the pope's or parson's nose). Preening chickens take oil from this gland with their beaks and dress their feathers with it.

Another type of bone not found in other animals is the *medullary*, which includes the ribs, toes, and others. These bones store calcium, which the hen draws on to make eggshells when dietary calcium isn't sufficient. (Eggshells are made primarily of calcium.)

Despite these significant differences, many similarities remain between avian and mammalian skeletons. The main difference between the bones of a chicken wing and a human arm is that the phalanges, or the bones that make up fingers and toes, are fused in chickens, so feathers can be attached. In legs, both species have a femur, fibula, and tibia. The next time you serve a chicken dinner, you can show off your vast knowledge of chickendom by asking your diners if they prefer the femur (thigh) or fibula/tibia (drumstick).

Respiratory System

As mentioned, chickens (and other birds) don't breathe like we mammals do. Their lungs are comparatively small and rigid and are firmly attached to the ribs; they don't inflate and deflate when the bird breathes. Instead, air is passed through the lungs by air sacs. These balloonlike structures force air through the lungs by compressing and distending, instead of the lungs doing the pumping. Chickens have nine such sacs, which are also connected to the air spaces in the pneumatic bones. Since the sacs collapse when the bird is slaughtered, most people who butcher chickens never see them, even though they fill a large proportion of the chest and abdominal cavity. An interesting and important side-note on pneumatic bones: a bird with a broken bone can have difficulty breathing when the bone is part of the respiratory system.

What all of this means to the chicken raiser is that chickens have a very sensitive breathing system and can be seriously affected by a dusty environment, a very humid one, ammonia in the air, and other signs of poor housekeeping.

About Crowing

Another part of the respiratory system that's of interest and importance to chicken raisers is the syrinx. The syrinx is located where the windpipe (trachea) separates into two branches and can be compared to the voice box (larynx) of mammals. Voice box equals crowing.

Every so often someone asks if it's possible to operate on a rooster—remove the syrinx—to eliminate crowing. No, it is not. However, crowing can be stopped by castration, or caponizing (which is not recommended by animal rights people, although others say it results in the most delectable roasters).

More often, someone is amazed to have a hen that crows. This isn't as unusual as it might seem and is easily explained. Hens have voice boxes, of course. And they're capable of crowing. The only reason they don't is because they don't feel like it. Really.

Crowing is a hormonal thing. Older hens, or those that undergo hormone changes because of diseased ovaries or other conditions, can experience a decrease in female hormones and an increase in male hormones, and they will often crow. Good luck explaining *that* if your hen starts crowing in a "no rooster" zone!

> ### Cacklings
>
> You will probably never take a chicken's pulse or temperature, but in case anybody ever asks ...
>
> The normal temperature of a chicken is around 107°F. A rooster breathes about 18 to 21 times a minute while a hen breathes about 31 to 35 times a minute. Heartbeat ranges from about 286 times a minute in males to 312 in females, when at rest.

Crowing contests are often popular events at fairs with poultry exhibits—the winner being the rooster who crows the most during a given period. However, some breeders also prize long-crowing roosters, especially in Japan, and several breeds have been developed to enhance this trait.

About Feathers

A chicken without feathers would be—well, pretty doggone ugly. Such a creature actually was developed in Israel a few years ago. A less drastic example is the *Naked Neck* chicken, a breed that is naturally devoid of feathers on the neck and vent. Conversely, feathers comprise a major part of the beauty of most birds. An investigation of feathers can result in a greater appreciation of that beauty, and at the same time uncover some interesting surprises.

def•i•ni•tion

The **Naked Neck** chicken, also called Transylvanian Naked Neck and Turken (because of its resemblance to the turkey), originated in Hungary and was developed in Germany. Common in Europe, Naked Necks are rare in the United States.

Strong Yet Flexible

Bird feathers evolved from reptilian scales. They not only "clothe" and insulate the bird, but they're essential for flight and courtship displays. Feathers grow from "feather buds" or *papillae* (Latin for pimples, which is what they look like) that appear on the fifth day of embryonic development. Even though birds are mostly covered with feathers, they all grow from "feather tracts," which are specific areas of the body.

Feathers are made of keratin, which is a fibrous protein that is also a main ingredient in horns, hoofs, claws, beaks, scales, and your own epidermis, hair, and nails. The keratin is what makes your outer layer of skin tough, compared to the inner layers. Where serious toughness is called for by rubbing and pressure, the number of cells containing keratin increases, resulting in a callus. Cells containing keratin are constantly being shed and replaced by new ones. When this occurs on the scalp, the result is dandruff.

In other words, keratin is pretty common and useful, something like nature's all-purpose plastic. Feathers are a perfect example.

These marvelous structures are strong enough to protect the bird, yet flexible.

Although all feathers might appear to be basically the same, there are several different kinds, each with a different purpose. And of course, to a bird lover, feathers are beautiful. But there's much more to them than meets the eye.

The various feather patterns—barred, stippled, penciled, spangled, laced, mottled—combined with the wide range of colors—golden, silver, black, blue, red, slate— means that backyard chickens can be as beautiful as any flower garden.

(Photo: Shana Reiley, Theresa, New York)

The fuzzy fluff on chicks is actually a form of feather called "natal downs." As the bird grows, other feathers appear: the contour feathers, which include flight feathers; rectrices or tail feathers; and coverts, which cover other feathers.

Feather Structure

The basic structure of a feather is easily seen in one of the long wing feathers, or flights. It seems to be a quill with some feathery stuff attached along two sides. The quill, or central shaft, is divided into two parts. The calamus is the part closest to the bird's body. It's hollow and doesn't have any vanes (the feathery stuff). The other, longer end of the shaft is the rachis, which is solid, and the part to which the vanes are attached. The narrower vane is the leading edge during flight and is called the outer vane. The wider part is the inner vane.

Vanes are made up of a series of parallel branches called barbs. At the ends of the barbs are short branchlets called barbules, which have microscopic hooks (barbicels) that lock the whole complex arrangement together, giving the feather great strength despite its light weight.

You have probably rubbed a feather the wrong way, getting it all mussed up, but rub it the right way, and presto, it's as good as new. That's because the barbicel hooks hold the vane together, much like Velcro. In fact, they hold it so tightly it makes the feather waterproof. (It's this tightness, and not oil, that makes water run off a duck's back.) Rubbing the feather the wrong way unhooks the barbicels.

Birds are also kept dry by contour feathers, which are the outermost ones. They generally overlap like shingles on a roof, shedding rain. Contour feathers determine the shape and color of the bird, and each can be controlled by a specialized set of muscles that allow the bird to "fluff" her feathers after mating or a dust bath.

Wing feathers are contour feathers that are strong and stiff, since they support the bird in flight. Most birds, anyway. No chicken can soar like an eagle, but some can't even get off the ground. The lighter breeds, such as Leghorns, can fly much better than the heavy breeds, such as Cornish. Nevertheless, they all have primaries, the largest and strongest of the wing feathers, which are attached to the wrist and finger (metacarpal and phalangeal) bones at the tip of the wing; secondaries, which are shorter and attached to the ulna in the middle of the wing; and tertiaries, the flight feathers closest to the body.

Tail feathers (retrices) are in another class, and coverts are the shorter and softer feathers that border and overlay the larger wing and tail feathers, adding streamlining and insulation. Down feathers are small, soft, and fluffy because they lack barbules and barbicel hooklets. Powder down feathers are special in that the ends disintegrate into a fine, talclike keratin powder, which the bird spreads over its feathers as it preens, as a cleaning and waterproofing agent.

Cocktail Conversation

The Onagadori chicken, a Japanese breed that doesn't exist in North America, has a tail that can be 12 feet long! Such growth is possible because of a nonmolting gene: the feathers just keep on growing, instead of being shed and replaced. The birds are housed in special coops called *tomebako* to protect those feathers. Handlers take them for daily exercise walks by holding the tail like a bridal train.

Other Uses for Feathers

Researchers are looking for ways to utilize the 2 to 4 billion pounds of feathers generated by poultry slaughterhouses every year, often in ways that reduce the need for petroleum. One example is synthetic fabric. (The keratin of feathers is the same type of fiber found in wool.) Walter Schmidt, a chemist with the Agricultural Research Service (ARS) in Beltsville, Maryland, has made a study of feathers. So far he has tinkered with chicken feather fiber to make paper, cloth, plant pots, diapers, insulation, and air filters, as well as mixing keratin and fiberglass to make boats and canoes and with plastic to mold into many other items such as auto dashboards.

At the University of Delaware, Richard Wool is director of the Affordable Composites from Affordable Resources (ACRES) program. Here the chicken emphasis is on using feathers to produce circuit boards. A conventional circuit board is basically a thin sheet of plastic covered with an even thinner sheet of copper foil. The unwanted copper is removed by chemical etching, leaving those fingerlike designs. This process consumes copper and petroleum and uses other chemicals such as chlorine. Eventually the copper is recovered, but the plastic is burned in the process. Feathers, or keratin, however, are biodegradable, and the soybean oil also used in the process is a renewable resource. The process isn't necessarily cheaper than conventional methods at this time, researchers say, but it's much more planet-friendly, which might be even more important.

You obviously don't have to know any of this to raise a chicken. But then, I've been saying that if you live in Key West or Kauai, you don't need to know *anything* to have chickens in your backyard. I think every one of these little details makes chickens, and for that matter all birds, very special. The mechanics of knowing how to raise a chicken are fine, helpful, and for some people necessary. But if your chickens mean more to you than eggs, meat, or money, the mechanics are a small part of raising them. Go ahead: I dare you to pick up a feather anytime in the future without testing the barbicels and being amazed at what you have just learned!

The Least You Need to Know

- Birds are descended from dinosaurs.
- Chickens have eight different types of combs.
- Lacking teeth, chickens grind their feed with the aid of little stones in their gizzard.
- Some of a chicken's bones are hollow, and some are part of its breathing system.
- Feathers are made of keratin, nature's all-purpose plastic.

Chapter 7

Understanding Chicken Behavior

In This Chapter

- Chicken behavior within the flock
- Roosting, preening, dust bathing, and other behaviors
- The language of chickens
- Training your chicken

Chickens are not dumb animals or birdbrains. They are social creatures, with a hierarchy and their own "language." They have the intelligence and memory of a young child and can be trained. Understanding even a little of chicken behavior can make keeping a few even more fun, interesting, and rewarding.

The Social Life of the Chicken

Wild chickens gather in flocks of up to 30. This accounts for many of their behavior patterns, which quickly become familiar to the new poultry keeper even with only three or four birds. They leave the henhouse, eat, drink, take dust baths, and roost as a group. Some will even nest and hatch eggs together. They are truly social animals. As such, and much like humans, they sometimes squabble.

The Pecking Order

Almost everyone is familiar with one aspect of flock behavior, because it's so often applied to more than chickens: *pecking order*. Some individuals simply dominate others, in descending rank. In chickens, pecking order starts at six to eight weeks of age with a variety of behaviors including attack, escape, and avoidance, leading to dominance and submissiveness. Researchers have found that a chicken can recognize more than a hundred other chickens, and remember them.

def•i•ni•tion

Pecking order refers to a hierarchy of social organization. It occurs in many animals, but since it was first described in chickens in 1921 the name has stuck, even when applied to humans.

After the pecking order has been established, it's accepted by all, and peace reigns: every chicken knows its place. Notice how the lower-ranking individuals keep their heads lower than the dominant ones. If they ever forget, or dare to relax that submissive posture, look out! Any nearby higher-ranking birds will quickly remind them of their place in the hierarchy.

Normally, roosters establish a hierarchy among themselves and generally dominate hens in a passive way, without fighting. Hens form their own social order on top of that. Larger combs confer higher rank, giving the birds that sport them an advantage in mixed flocks. However, introducing a new bird or birds causes havoc, since the hierarchy has to be established all over again. Don't change the flock structure by introducing new birds frequently. Frequent changes cause unnecessary strife, and stress of any kind can lead to lower disease resistance.

If you do bring a new chicken into the flock, it's best to do it gradually, preferably at dusk, or perhaps by separating the newcomer in a cage where all the birds can see each other but without physical contact. The outcome of introducing new birds is variable. Some chickens are much more sociable and tolerant of newcomers than others. Even so, the pecking order is natural and is to be expected, so be prepared.

Under normal circumstances the pecking order is no problem for either the chickens or the caretakers. But if there is a shortage of feed, water, or roosting space, the hens lowest on the social ladder will be the first to suffer.

Very often, birds of a feather stick together. In mixed flocks it's common for birds to prefer the company of others of their own breed, or even color. Although most roosters have "favorite" hens, many tend to pay more attention to their own kind.

Foraging Behavior

Wild chickens spend most of their time foraging. (One authority pins it down to 61 percent.) Although the walking, scratching, and pecking imply searching for food and water, chickens seem driven to forage even when provided with adequate food. The significance of this for chicken raisers is that hens in an environment that hinders foraging behavior show signs of stress, such as feather picking. No doubt about it, chickens simply love to wander around looking for something to eat, which is impossible in a cage.

> **Cocktail Conversation**
>
> Chickens find food by scratching with their strong feet and claws and pecking with their horny beaks. Someone has determined that a chicken pecks 10,000 times a day. I don't know whether to be more amazed by that number, or by the thought of somebody actually bothering to count something like that.

Nesting Behavior

Before laying an egg, a hen leaves the flock and searches for a suitable nesting site. Most often this means a darkened, somewhat protected out-of-the-way spot, although many young hens have no compunctions about laying an egg in the middle of the hen-house floor, or anywhere else, for that matter. If straw or some other nesting material is provided, she spends time arranging it to her satisfaction.

According to Dr. Ian Duncan of the Department of Animal and Poultry Sciences at the University of Guelph, Ontario, and a leading expert on chicken behavior, the inability of caged egg-laying hens to make a nest is their greatest single source of frustration.

Several hens will share one nest, often at the same time. Some take it even further, hatching eggs together, and then raising the brood communally. However, hens seeing strange chicks for the first time have been known to go after them, even killing them. Chickens can be unpredictable, just like people.

Hens often share a nest— even at the same time.

(Photo: Jeanne Griffin, Lexington, South Carolina)

Roosting

In nature, roosting in trees protects chickens from ground predators, and again, this behavior is so engrained that confined birds become agitated at dusk if no roosts are available. Roosts allow submissive birds to avoid dominant ones, making bedtime more peaceful. Chickens' feet are adapted to close around a perch when they sit so they cling tightly, even when asleep.

A roost can be incorporated even into a small coop.

(Photo: April Shotick, Medina, Ohio)

Preening

Preening is another typical chicken behavior. Preening occurs when a chicken spreads oil (secreted by a gland near the tail) over the feathers to keep them supple and water-resistant. During molt, preening might indicate irritation of the feather follicles. The amount and staleness of the oil on the feathers can stimulate another chicken behavior, dust bathing.

Dust Bathing

One of the more picturesque activities of your backyard flock is taking dust baths. They especially like soft, loose soil—such as where you just planted flowers.

Chickens love to take dust baths, especially in nice, fluffy flower beds. The dust removes excess oil from the feathers and inhibits skin parasites.

(Photo: Joanna Wilcox, Boone, North Carolina)

Little boys in particular are intrigued by the thought of taking a bath by rolling in the dirt. For chickens, the dry dust maintains feather condition by dispersing oils and inhibiting skin parasites. Hens on free range spend a lot of time dust bathing, usually in a group, and in favored spots that become wallows. Ours have always had a preference for close to the house foundation (flowers, again) where the ground is usually bare and dry. Some observers have concluded that the inability to bathe, like the inability to forage, leads to chicken psychosis. Many breeders provide a box containing sand or soil, often mixed with sifted wood ashes, for their chickens' feather and mental health.

Chicken Talk

Chickens communicate. Watch and listen to chickens carefully for even a brief period, and you'll be amazed at their range of clucks and cackles, or chirping and crowing. We're told that they make some 30 different sounds, with different meanings. If you pay close attention, it won't take long to understand some of them. Your first day-old chicks readily let you know if they're hot, cold, hungry, or perfectly content, not only by their actions but by vocalization. Actually, chicks start "talking" even before they hatch—at least if there is a mother hen to start the conversation. Both hens and roosters make different sounds regarding big birds overhead, approaching dogs or foxes, or the discovery of a particularly delectable tidbit.

You don't have to spend a lot of time around chickens to be convinced that they communicate. These Buff Orpingtons appear to be having a serious discussion.

(Photo: Gale Miko, New Jersey)

Interestingly, after centuries of debate, no one seems to have a believable scientific explanation of why a hen cackles after laying an egg. The anthropomorphic translation to "Look what I just did!" has many skeptics. The contention that she's drawing attention away from her nest doesn't hold much water, either: we frequently find eggs in hidden nests by paying attention to where a hen is cackling!

Aggression

As with people, individual chickens can vary greatly in every respect. There are also breed differences. Aggression provides a good example.

Roosters are naturally more aggressive than hens, but some roosters are much more aggressive than others. Some people have been scarred for life after being attacked by a rooster as children; others have found lifelong enjoyment in raising chickens after having a gentle rooster as a childhood pet.

We have had several Rhode Island Red roosters attack men, women, children, dogs, and motorcycles. (Roosters have spurs, which are horny growths on the back of their legs that can inflict serious damage.) Then we have had huge Light Brahma roosters that were calm and friendly. And some roosters discriminated between men and women, or adults and children, or became vicious only in certain situations.

> **Fox Alert**
>
> An attack rooster is akin to a mean-tempered pit bull and not to be tolerated. They certainly have no place where children might be present or in an urban setting.

Chicken Tricks and Training

Chickens are easily trained. I'm surprised we don't hear more about this, with so many people raising them as pets nowadays. Sixty years ago we had a neighbor with a bantam rooster named Davey, who did back flips on command. Variety shows in the early days of television often featured chickens that could perform tricks, often involving pecking at something, but also such tasks as pulling a bread pan by an attached string. Today, trainers of dogs and other animals, often for advertisements or movies, learn their craft by training chickens.

I can envision a public meeting debating whether or not chickens should be allowed in a certain town, where the pro-chicken people put on a demonstration. Imagine this: a chicken climbs a small ladder to a foot-wide platform. Turning 180 degrees, it continues across a narrow bridge, like a tight-rope, to another platform. It pecks at a tethered ping-pong ball, winding it around its post. Ignoring the amused spectators, the bird turns again, descends a second ladder back to the ground, and encounters two bowling pins. It knocks down the yellow one first and then the blue one. Applause.

This scenario was the assigned task at workshops conducted by Bob Bailey and his psychologist wife, Marian Breland-Bailey, at a "chicken training camp." The training was accomplished in five days of 60- to 90-minute sessions. The goal was not to train chickens, but to train people—to train animals of all kinds. Marian and her first husband, Keller Breland, worked with noted psychologist B. F. Skinner and were instrumental in training pigeons and dolphins for military purposes in World War II. The later focus was on dogs and other animals, but they continued to use chickens to train the trainers. The technique became known as "operant conditioning." This includes such principles as behavior shaping. You start with a simple behavior the animal readily offers—such as pecking—and gradually develop that into your goal, such as knocking a tethered ping-pong ball around a post.

Marian died in 2001, and Bob discontinued the classes in 2004, but as of early 2009, their website was still up, containing some helpful and interesting information about animal training and operant conditioning. See www.hsnp.com/behavior/index.html.

The idea of "training the trainer" is an important concept around animals of any kind. Children in particular should be made aware of their effect on animals. Chickens, like certain grumpy old men, will not remain calm around rowdy children. Both children and adults should be trained to move slowly and deliberately when feeding or watering birds, gathering eggs, or simply observing them. Avoid sudden moves and loud noises. As one experienced mother said, children should use their "inside voice" around the chickens. It's only logical that chickens being chased or teased, either by dogs or children, will be stressed—and roosters will become defensive. Firm rules about proper behavior in the vicinity of the chicken coop must be laid down and enforced from the beginning.

The Least You Need to Know

- ◆ Chickens are social creatures, roosting together and often sharing a nest.

- ◆ Great variation in temperament and behavior exists between breeds, and even more between individuals.

- ◆ Chickens supposedly have a "vocabulary" of 30 different meaningful sounds.

- ◆ Chickens can be trained to perform tricks.

Chapter 8

Health Concerns

In This Chapter

- ◆ The small-flock advantage
- ◆ Diseases and parasites to be aware of
- ◆ Zoonoses concerns
- ◆ Biosecurity for the small flock

A farmer with a thousand chickens is a thousand times more likely to have a sick chicken than is a backyarder with one chicken. That doesn't prevent some small-flock owners from worrying about illnesses. Let's address some of their concerns.

Most Chickens Are Healthy

You'd expect chickens to be healthy. After all, they don't smoke, drink, stay out late, overeat, or have any of the other bad habits blamed for most human ailments. But even clean living is no defense against illness. As Dr. W. F. Landskron (my father-in-law) often said, "Everybody has to die of *something*." Most of the world's 24 billion chickens do not die a natural death or from disease.

Cacklings

My colleague Gail Damerow and I are both farmers and former magazine editors who wrote *Storey's Guide to Raising* ... books, plus others. She has been accused of placing too much emphasis on diseases. I have been accused of ignoring them.

It seems to me that some people (not Gail!) are obsessed by disease and sickness; they waste money, worry unnecessarily, and don't enjoy life with their animals as they should. If you don't care for my approach, Gail's *The Chicken Health Handbook* (Garden Way Publishing/Storey Communications, Inc., 1994) will certainly fill the gap.

This wasn't always the case. In the early years of mass-produced poultry products, entire flocks were wiped out by disease. Chickens didn't take kindly to being confined together in flocks of thousands. And of course, under those crowded conditions, when one got sick, they all got sick.

Scientific inquiry into diseases and antibiotics was increasing at the same time chickens were first being mass-produced. Pasteur's first successful vaccine, for chicken cholera, was accidentally discovered in 1880, but the disease was still widespread 50 years later. Milo Hastings was one of the first proponents of raising chickens on a grand scale. He wrote a book about it (*The Dollar Hen*, 1911), unsuccessfully tried to patent a huge incubator, and for more than a decade was quite free with his untested advice on the subject. By 1928 he had 10,000 layers in Tarrytown, New York. That's the year penicillin, the first antibiotic, was discovered, but it was too late to help Hastings. In 1929 cholera wiped out his entire flock in a matter of weeks, and that's the last we heard of his involvement with poultry.

New discoveries and applications in poultry nutrition and feed formulation mushroomed at the same time as the discovery of antibiotics, with obvious implications for chicken health. Without these technologies, egg and broiler factories probably never would have gotten off the ground, and all chicken meat and eggs would still come from backyard flocks and small farms. The big operations couldn't function without these scientific technologies; the small ones rarely need them.

Medicated Feeds

Why are antibiotics used, what do they do, and what's the problem with them? Often referred to as "growth enhancers," they are added to feed in low amounts to nip disease problems in the bud. They enhance growth, not because of their inherent chemical properties but because they suppress disease-causing bacteria that would otherwise *inhibit* growth. This is a prophylactic, or preventive, use of drugs, in contrast to therapeutic, or curative use.

The Creation of "Superbugs"

The major problem concerns bugs that develop immunity to specific antibiotics, and become the so-called "superbugs" now being seen among humans, particularly in hospitals. The viral mutations are attributed mostly to nontherapeutic livestock use of antibiotics: nearly 25 million pounds a year, or more than eight times as much as is used for human medical use. According to the Centers for Disease Control (CDC), 17 classes of antimicrobials are approved for food animal growth promotion in the United States. When the bugs become more resistant to these drugs fed to healthy chickens and other animals, the drugs become less effective when used to treat sick humans.

Start with Healthy Stock

With so much emphasis on prevention, a sick chicken is rare. And with the potential for economic catastrophe from a disease outbreak, that rare sick chicken is made rarer by immediate disposal, including incineration. The whole secret of poultry health, then, is to start out with healthy birds, and keep them that way. Curing a sick chicken is seldom on option.

Starting out with healthy chicks or chickens is most easily accomplished by buying them from a reputable source, such as an established hatchery. Then keep them that way with proper nutrition and sanitation. Add to that the fact that "enhanced growth" is not an issue with backyard flocks (see Chapter 12), and you'll find no need or reason to use medicated feeds.

Medicated feeds contain antibiotics in very low (prophylactic) amounts to prevent minor diseases and promote faster, more efficient growth. For birds that are actually sick, higher (therapeutic) levels are usually given in water or injected into the bird, not mixed with the feed. Common antibiotics include penicillin, bacitracin, chlortetracycline, and oxytetracycline.

Unmedicated feeds are available. In fact, medicated feeds must have warning labels indicating withdrawal times; that is, the period during which nonmedicated feeds must be fed before eating the eggs or meat. Some people equate unmedicated feeds with organic feeds. The two aren't the same, but so far as what most people are concerned about—that is, the antibiotics—there is no difference, because neither has them.

It's not difficult to tell when a chicken isn't feeling up to par. A healthy bird is active and perky, bright-eyed, and glossy-feathered. If it acts droopy, there's a reason. If its eyes are dull, the feathers dull and ruffled, or it breathes noisily, something's wrong. By that time it's probably too late to do much about it. Balancing the value and productive life span of a chicken against the cost and uncertain results of treating it, most people believe all the chicken medicine cabinet needs is a hatchet and a chopping block. (See Chapter 13 for other means of euthanizing birds.)

Cocktail Conversation

Chicken mortality is high in lesser-developed areas, where eggs are hatched by hens, vaccines and other medications are rare, predators are common, and the birds survive (if they do) largely by scavenging. As an experiment, the veterinary faculty at the University of Yucatan in Mexico distributed 10 to 12 three-week-old chicks to 24 randomly selected families in one village. Three months later, 43 percent of the birds were dead. The two leading causes were coccidiosis and Marek's Disease (see the following section). Both are routinely treated with preventive medicine in the United States.

Diseases to Be Aware Of

The most common small-flock chicken health problems don't involve disease at all, according to Elaine Belanger, editor of *Backyard Poultry* magazine. In fact, the leading calls for help concern feather loss—which in most cases is due to the activity of roosters! (Some hens' backs are totally devoid of feathers due to roosters' claws.) The second most common health-related matter involves scaly leg mites, which of course are parasites, not a disease. Perhaps ironically, while we often hear that small flocks are healthier than commercial flocks, neither of these are problems in caged, commercial operations. We'll talk about parasites later, but meanwhile, there are several diseases you will probably hear about, and presumably will want to know about, even though you're unlikely to encounter them in your own coop.

Marek's Disease

If you order chicks from a hatchery, the first disease you're likely to hear about is Marek's Disease, or MD. You should be aware of this because some hatcheries vaccinate all chicks for MD while others offer it at an extra cost.

MD is so widespread that some authorities say if you have chickens, they have MD. Even vaccination doesn't prevent infection, but it does prevent the tumors. There is no known cure or treatment. Yet, you are unlikely to see a case of MD because vaccination is almost universal.

MD is a type of avian cancer. It's highly contagious, and transmitted by air inside the poultry house containing chicken house dust—feather dander, excreta, and saliva. It affects mostly young birds. Unvaccinated chicks 10 to 12 weeks old can suffer 50 percent mortality. Symptoms can include paralysis of the legs or wings; diarrhea, weakness, and general depression; tumors on feather follicles; pale and shriveled comb; and blindness, often in one eye, leading to the synonym "gray eye."

Chicks must be vaccinated upon hatching, before they go into the brooder. If you hatch your own chicks you can vaccinate them yourself, but as of this writing, the smallest quantity of vaccine available is 200 doses, and any that is unused must be discarded; you can't save it from one hatch to another.

To summarize and repeat: you prevent MD with vaccination at hatching; there is no cure or treatment.

Pullorum

You are also sure to hear about pullorum, for two reasons. One is that most states now require blood-testing for this nonrespiratory bacterial disease before chickens are shown or sold. The other reason is that pullorum is a reportable disease: in most states it's mandatory that if one chicken has pullorum, the entire flock must be "depopulated"—destroyed—whether they're sick or not. The disease isn't a threat to humans, but it's one of the old-time ones that even today, theoretically, could wipe out the poultry industry. The good news is, it's very rare in North America.

Pullorum is usually spread from hen to chick, through the egg, but it can also be transmitted by contaminated incubators or houses and equipment. It affects chicks usually around five to seven days of age, beginning with huddling, droopiness, pasted vent, gasping, and chalk-white excreta that can be stained with green bile. If you suspect pullorum, contact a veterinarian, your cooperative extension agent, or the state veterinarian. (For a directory of all state vets, see http://agr.wa.gov/FoodAnimal/animalhealth/StateVets.aspx.) Again, there is no cure, and affected flocks must be destroyed. Outbreaks and eradication are handled by state/federal regulatory agencies.

Cocktail Conversation

A pullorum test unit can be had for around $150, with the required antigen stain another $125 or so. (The test involves drawing a blood sample.) These tests are now in common use at shows, fairs, and sales. As part of the National Poultry Improvement Plan (NPIP), testing breeder replacement flocks before the onset of production is mandatory. Testing includes chickens, turkeys, show birds, waterfowl, game birds, and guinea fowl.

Coccidiosis

Coccidiosis is an interesting disease because it's another one that home flocks are susceptible to, while caged birds are not. At the same time, it's considered one of the most expensive diseases encountered by the poultry industry because it's so common among broilers, which are raised on litter, not in cages. The disease is caused by protozoans (genus *Eimeria*) with a life cycle that involves stages both in the chicken's body and in litter, as *oocysts*. Most chick feed contains a *coccidiostat*, which controls the problem, but keeping litter dry and using plenty of it to dilute the oocysts, plus giving the birds enough space so they are exposed to fewer of them, should also do the job.

def•i•ni•tion

A **coccidiostat** is any one of a number of drugs, including sulfamethazine and amprolium, administered to prevent or treat coccidiosis. **Oocysts** are the eggs of certain parasites.

Other Diseases

As you might expect, we could talk about dozens of diseases, many with variations, all with varying symptoms and treatments. Under certain circumstances, some treatments can kill rather than cure. For example, the level of sulfamethazine used to treat coccidiosis is close to the level that can cause poisoning. The drug is added to water. In hot weather chickens drink more water, get more of the drug, and can die of poisoning. Multiply pesky details like that by a few dozen and it's easy to see that playing amateur doctor can be risky and is seldom worth the effort and expense.

Avian Veterinarians

Taking a sick chicken to a veterinarian is possible, but most unusual. A primary reason is that the vet bill is almost certain to be more than the chicken is worth. (Like people doctors and lawyers, veterinarians do not appreciate phone calls from people looking for free advice.) In addition, few vets know very much about chickens. Many of them, like most poultry raisers, are of the opinion that the only items required in a poultry medicine cabinet are a hatchet and a chopping block.

Fox Alert

A chicken that appears to be sick or doesn't act right should be isolated, to protect the rest of the flock. Do what you can to get it to eat and drink, and make it comfortable. If you have a suspicion of what the problem might be and can find any advice about correcting it, try it. If the chicken doesn't improve within a few days, the best course is to cull it (see Chapter 13).

Poultry Parasites

External parasites can be a minor nuisance or a serious problem, depending on the numbers, but obviously, a slight infestation can become a major plague if not detected and controlled. Control usually means treating the house and equipment as well as the birds.

Fortunately, these pests can usually be seen with a thorough examination. When you hug your chicken each day, check for lice and mites at the same time.

Lice

First, the good news. Poultry lice are host-specific. That means they won't transfer to you or your dog.

Several species of lice affect poultry, but they are all tiny, wingless, flat-bodied insects (six-legged). A female louse will lay 50 to 300 eggs at a time, usually cementing them near the base of a feather shaft. Unlike most lice, those living on poultry don't suck blood: they live on dry skin scales, feathers, and scabs.

Most infestations start in the vent area. Look for live, light brown or straw-colored lice crawling on the bird, and for the white eggs, or nits. Chewed feathers might look raggedy, or moth-eaten.

Chickens get lice from other chickens or wild birds, so prevention includes carefully checking any newcomers to the flock and keeping out wild birds. Control requires an insecticide approved for use on poultry. Be sure your chickens have access to a dust bath, which will also help.

Mites

Several different mites affect poultry, each with slightly different life cycles, habits, and effects. However, two of the most common in small flocks are closely related: scaly leg mites, and depluming mites.

Scaly leg mites are tiny, round, and flat. They burrow under the scales of the feet and lower legs, raising the scales and making the legs look deformed. Some authorities advise dipping the legs in linseed oil, wiping them clean, then coating them with petroleum jelly. Others say just rubbing in the petroleum jelly is sufficient. Both agree that the old-time remedies of kerosene or other petroleum products are a no-no. The life cycle of the scaly leg mite is two weeks, so treatment should be repeated once or twice weekly for several weeks.

Depluming mites are found on the skin, at the base of feather shafts. Their feeding causes intense itching, which results in the chicken pecking at the mites and even pulling out its own feathers. This can lead to bacterial skin infections, and even cannibalism, as other chickens are attracted to the bloodied area. There is no officially approved insecticide for these pests, but permethrin spray and dust treatments are commonly used. Kansas State University suggests looking for it as Permectrin Dairy Cattle and Swine Dust; or as a spray, Atroban, Ectiban, Insectaban, Insectrin, or Permectrin II. Ohio State University says severe infestations can be treated with a kitten-strength dose of a pyrethrin-based medicated spray.

def•i•ni•tion

Diatomaceous earth (DE) is a soft, chalklike sedimentary rock consisting of fossilized diatoms, a form of hard-shelled algae. It's commonly used in swimming pool filters and industrial processes, and as an organic insecticide and pest control. Be sure to use a food grade, not a swimming pool product, around chickens.

External parasites can be introduced to a flock by wild birds and at poultry shows, or by bringing in new birds. Wild birds should be kept away from chickens, and show birds and new birds should be isolated and observed for two weeks before being housed with the flock. Keys to controlling mites and lice are cleanliness and sanitation, which includes disinfecting the coop and equipment if parasites are noticed. Sunshine is the best disinfectant. After that, providing a box for dust baths containing sifted wood ashes, dry soil, and food-grade *diatomaceous earth* (DE) will be helpful.

Chickens and Human Health

A disease that can be transferred from an animal to a human is called a zoonosis. Of the few chicken diseases that carry a risk of human infection, that risk is mostly rated low, very low, or extremely low. Two that carry a moderate risk are campylobacteriosis and salmonellosis. However, in both cases the danger comes not from raising chickens or being around them, but in eating chickens or eggs that are not adequately cooked. In other words, the risk is about the same whether you raise chickens, or just consume poultry products without ever coming into contact with live birds.

Chickens don't have a monopoly on either disease, but the warnings of the dangers of raw chicken led celebrity chef Emeril Lagasse to joke about "the chicken police" who want you to disinfect everything raw chicken comes in contact with, including the car you brought it home in. The jokes reinforced a simple truth: raw chicken is a leading source of food-borne illness. That doesn't mean it's the *only* one. Other meats, raw milk, contaminated water, and household pets are also sources, as well as infected humans who don't thoroughly wash their hands. I repeat: the problem is not from raising chickens, but from raw and undercooked meat and eggs.

Campylobacter

According to the CDC, 47 percent of raw chicken breasts tested were contaminated with campylobacter germs. A single drop of infected chicken blood on a cutting board can contaminate any raw foods prepared on the board, such as salad.

Campylobacteriosis is an infectious intestinal disease—food poisoning—caused by bacteria of the genus *Campylobacter*. Common symptoms can include diarrhea, cramping, abdominal pain, and fever within two to five days after exposure to the organism. The diarrhea might be bloody and can be accompanied by nausea and vomiting. The illness usually lasts a week.

Salmonella

Salmonellosis is also a type of food poisoning, with similar effects on the digestive system, but this one is generally associated with fecal matter. It can be spread by direct contact, but tracing it is sometimes difficult, as illustrated by the recent case of growing vegetables contaminated by irrigation water. Some people fault highly automated slaughtering plants, where, well before the end of a shift, a carcass might be "washed" and cooled in water high in fecal matter.

Children who don't wash their hands after playing with chicks—or turtles, puppies, or many other animals (and anyone else who puts their germ-laden hands near their mouths)—can become infected with salmonella. Children under five are five times more likely than the general population to get salmonellosis. Remember to tell your children that, after going potty or playing with animals, they must wash their hands with soap for at least as long as it takes to sing the birthday song.

Avoiding food-borne germs isn't easy today, but preventing the diseases they spread is quite simple. Avoid raw eggs and unpasteurized milk. Keep foods, including eggs, refrigerated. Wash hands with soap and water both before and after handling any raw meat. Avoid cross-contamination by using separate cutting boards for meat and other foods, and carefully scrub cutting boards, countertops, and utensils with soap and hot water. Chicken must be cooked to a minimum internal temperature of 165°F, and eggs must be cooked at 145°F for 3½ minutes. (Egg whites coagulate at 144°F to 149°F, so sunnyside-up eggs are not government approved.)

Avian Flu

Bird flu, or avian influenza A (H5N1), was big news a few years ago. The United States Department of Health, Education and Welfare says there is no need at present to remove a flock of chickens because of concerns regarding avian influenza. The U.S. Department of Agriculture monitors potential infection of poultry and poultry products by avian influenza viruses and other infectious disease agents (see www.cdc.gov/flu/avian/gen-info/qa.htm).

The United Nations World Health Organization's website at www.who.int/csr/disease/avian_influenza/updates/en/index.html updates the bird flu situation regularly. The listings I skimmed through were mostly from Asia or the Middle East and involved children who "had confirmed contact with sick and dead chickens."

Cocktail Conversation

Chickenpox has nothing to do with chickens. The disease *varicella* got that name supposedly because somebody thought the blisters accompanying it looked like chickpeas.

There has not been a single case of avian flu in the United States—not in domestic poultry, wild birds, or humans. According to experts such as the Pew Commission on Farm Animal Production, if avian flu does appear here, it will most likely be in large commercial flocks. In a 2006 report, GRAIN, an international sustainable agriculture group, concluded that when it comes to bird flu, diverse small-scale poultry farming isn't a problem: it's the solution.

Practice Biosecurity

Diseases can be spread. Biosecurity is a management system to prevent your healthy chickens from coming into contact with the agents that can cause disease.

In large, commercial installations, traffic is strictly controlled. In most, visitors aren't allowed. Feed trucks and other vehicles are disinfected. Avoiding contamination from outside sources is taken very, very seriously.

Similar advice about traffic is often given to the backyarder, although obviously less risk is involved. However, most coop tours and similar open houses require visitors to wear booties or to go through a disinfectant foot bath when going from one poultry setting to another. It's just a commonsense precaution.

Another aspect of biosecurity pertains to bringing in new birds, or even returning your own from a show where they might have been exposed to disease. It's common practice to isolate and observe such chickens for two weeks, just to be sure.

Wild birds are a more common problem for the average small flock. Avian influenza has been linked to migrating wild birds, and pigeons, starlings, and sparrows can transmit disease. Keeping them away from your chickens, and their feed, is an essential part of biosecurity.

The Least You Need to Know

◆ Start with healthy birds, feed them right, practice good sanitation, and you're unlikely to ever encounter a sick chicken.

◆ Most small flocks have a bigger problem with mites and lice than with diseases.

◆ Food-related health issues connected with poultry and eggs can be averted by proper cooking and by avoiding cross-contamination.

◆ To avoid exposing your chickens to parasites or disease, isolate any new birds for two weeks and examine them carefully before integrating them into your flock.

Chapter 9

Crowds and Flocks

In This Chapter

- ◆ Legitimate concerns about city poultry
- ◆ How to minimize nuisances
- ◆ Illegal avians: the underground approach to city poultry keeping
- ◆ Manure: a valuable byproduct

Chickens can be content living almost anywhere: in the jungle, on farms, in urban and suburban backyards, even in vacant city lots and rooftop gardens. Again, it's humans who complicate things. Nowhere does it get more complicated than in towns and cities, where people flock as closely together as roosting chickens.

When Poultry Presents Problems

Anyone who wants to raise a chicken can usually do so with no questions asked. But where people live closely crammed together, especially when some of them are sharply divorced from nature and the realities of life, the presence of poultry can become a problem.

Fear of Chickens

Some people suffer from *alektorophobia*—the fear of chickens. (*Alector* is Greek for "rooster.") As with most phobias, this fear can result from an early traumatic experience, such as being attacked by a rooster. However, some cases have been attributed to such simple events as news coverage of the tragic conditions in which modern factory-raised chickens live and die, or even just hearing about diseases related to chickens. Severe cases can actually affect the victim's ability to function in the normal world.

As with most phobias, treatment can include hypnotherapy and exposure therapy—meaning the patient overcomes the fear by becoming acquainted with a chicken.

Separation of Town and Country

Alektorophobia is rare. Much more common is the person who firmly believes that the distinction between town and country should be as clearly divided, and as complete and final, as the separation of church and state. This group undoubtedly includes many who think food is manufactured in the back room of their local supermarket, and those who consider all animals stupid, smelly, and unsanitary.

Roosters, Pests, and Odor

A third group has a more realistic and reasonable outlook. They are justifiably upset by the thought of roosters crowing in the morning—and will become even more irritated if or when they discover that to most roosters, "morning" can come long before the sun rises and often lasts all day. They are concerned that poultry, and poultry feed, might attract rodents and other pests. And what about odors?

Roosters are loud!

(Photo: Karen and Abby Sandstrom, Hebron, Connecticut)

Roosters have been mentioned and pictured frequently in these pages, with affection, admiration, and the firm conviction that they don't belong in the city. I have made the mistake of locating the chicken coop too close to my bedroom window, and that was on a 160-acre farm! I shudder to even think about what it must be like where there are three or four houses per acre. Combined with their potentially pugnacious nature—remember, we first bred chickens for their fighting ability, not for their meat or eggs—we must, perhaps regretfully, exclude the cock from the urban backyard flock.

Roosters are beautiful but unwanted in most densely populated areas.

(Photo: Jane Mallory, Corinth, Kentucky)

Those with the phobia might rate our pity, but most of them would be as traumatized by a KFC as by a Rhode Island Red. They need professional help. The **second** group is a product of modern affluenza and its disconnect with nature and the real world. They're the ones who go storming to the city authorities when a neighbor dares to convert a lawn into a natural prairie. (I even met one who complained about his neighbor "destroying the neighborhood" by planting a packet of sweet corn seeds in his backyard. "Grow corn in the country, where it belongs," he huffed.) These are people who would fly into a rage at the soft and gentle cluck of a contented hen—who get upset by cooing mourning doves—but who have no problem with early-morning roars and whines of lawn mowers and leaf blowers. Fortunately (or hopefully), it's the third group we most often encounter: reasonable, intelligent people with legitimate concerns.

Now we get down to the nitty-gritty: what about odors—and rodents?

Reducing Nuisances

I assume that you don't want to live in a stinking rat-infested place any more than your neighbors do. That doesn't automatically eliminate poultry-keeping. All it requires is a little planning, work, and common sense. (Much too often, all three are lacking even among dog and cat owners.)

Manure Management

Farm books tell us chickens excrete 4.5 tons of manure a year per 1,000 pounds live-weight. That's 9 pounds of manure per pound of live chicken. From that we deduce that a typical hen weighing 7 pounds produces 63 pounds of poop a year. (Much of that weight is water.)

Logic lesson #1: this amounts to 189 pounds for three birds, but twice that much for six, and three times as much for nine. Any litter, or bedding, is in addition to that. When you're talking about manure, more is not better, unless you have a large garden and/or are an expert composter. (We'll talk about that in a moment.) In other words, a city flock of three or four chickens might be much more manageable than a dozen or more, just on the basis of manure.

Chicken droppings that are kept dry with litter, and that are cleaned up and composted before they become offensive, are good for the owner, for neighbor relations, and for the chickens themselves. Frequency of cleaning depends on many factors including the weather (less in winter), the amount of space in an outside yard, and the type and amount of litter. Some people advocate "deep litter" housing systems. When the litter is 6 inches deep (or more) and turned frequently, the coop can be cleaned once a year. Others are meticulous about thorough cleaning and sanitizing weekly, or oftener. Most small coops are designed to be cleaned easily and frequently, and with a minimum of litter. For suggestions on what to do with the manure, keep reading.

Fly Control

Moist chicken droppings can attract flies. Flies can be controlled with fly traps. (They can't be *eliminated* with anything.) There are several different kinds of traps, all relatively inexpensive. For one site on how to build a no-cost trap, see http://insected. arizona.edu/flyrear.htm. Keep several in use, and start *before* the flies become a problem. For an entirely different slant on flies, see how one expert homesteader actually raises fly maggots to feed chickens at www.themodernhomestead.us/article/Feeding-Chickens-Maggots.html.

Rodents

Rats and mice are opportunists. They can be found anywhere, including tony neighborhoods that don't have chickens, but they're attracted by easy meals. Among the easiest are accessible stored feed and spilled feed. Both can be eliminated. Store feed in tightly covered metal containers, limit spillage by not overfilling feeders, and clean up any accidental spills that do occur. Just as importantly, eliminate any places or conditions that permit the pests to hide and breed. And finally, if there is the slightest chance of a rodent being present, don't hesitate even a minute to eliminate it by whatever means necessary. Both traps and poisons have limitations and can be dangerous if not properly used. Read and follow the manufacturer's directions carefully.

> **Fox Alert**
>
> If you're inclined to go soft on vermin, for whatever reason, just remember that one female rat can produce five litters a year—with an average of 7 but as many as 14 in a litter. And don't think that "a few" is okay. It's a biological fact that the reproduction rate goes up as the food supply increases, but also as population *decreases*. The fewer there are, the more urgently nature tries to fill the void.

Practice Public Relations

That's the good, the bad, and the ugly. Where does that leave you if you live in a city or town and want to raise chickens?

Jennifer Blecha wrote her doctoral dissertation on people's attitudes toward urban livestock, including chickens. She checked the zoning codes of 78 American cities and found that 53 allow hens and 16 prohibit them. Apparently, the question hasn't come up yet in the remaining nine: chickens aren't mentioned. That would seem to suggest that you can legally raise chickens in nearly 80 percent of American cities. But she noted that the trend is toward becoming more permissive, and that cities are generally more tolerant than suburbs.

If you know your neighbors well and are on good terms with them, you might just build a nice coop and get a few birds. Depending on proximity and landscaping, chances are that most of your neighbors will never even know. If they do, and they're in the "reasonable" class mentioned previously, they (and their children) will probably be as interested in the project as you are. And gifting a few fresh eggs now and then won't hurt a bit.

This underground approach is much more common than some people realize. A recent newspaper article mentioned a person who was pushing the law with her chickens, but she didn't want to be named because she was an attorney.

Until a few years ago most municipalities had no regulations regarding chickens, and many still don't. The subject just never came up. Some people would prefer to keep it that way. In 2008 the Worldwatch Institute reported that growing numbers of city dwellers were raising chickens, often in defiance of local ordinances.

Many people try to keep their chickens invisible. One way to hide them in plain sight is with this HenCondo Stephen Keel designed to look like a trash can. Would you believe this is a chicken coop? See this, and more of his coops, at http://henspa.com.

(Photo: Egganic Industries)

With the explosive growth in urban backyard flocks, more and more city councils are finding themselves debating chicken ordinances. In some cases the results are favorable. Ann Arbor, Michigan; Ft. Collins, Colorado; South Portland, Maine; and Madison, Wisconsin, are a few examples. Chickens are allowed, with the provisions we just mentioned as being reasonable: no roosters, limited numbers, and proper animal husbandry. Because these rules (if they exist) are different in every jurisdiction, and because they are changing so rapidly, it's impossible to give you any advice beyond checking with city hall. Interestingly, cities seem to be more lenient than suburbs. To get some idea of what's going on nationwide currently, visit http://home.centurytel.net/thecitychicken/chickenlaws.html or a more technical site, www.municode.com.

If the subject has come up recently in your city, you probably read about it in the newspaper, and are aware of the local situation. You can ask the city clerk or equivalent for information, but if there are any regulations, read them. City clerks sometimes have their own opinions and agendas, which can work for or against you. One well-known case, caught on audio tape and posted on YouTube, has several Chicago officials telling an aspiring chicken raiser that poultry is prohibited within the city limits, which is not true. The written ordinances, if they exist, are what count. But in many cases all it takes is a little discretion, especially if you know your neighbors and are on good terms with them.

The Democratic Way

What if your city officials are dominated by a few people with alektorophobia? Don't give up too easily. There have been cases in which opponents have been converted, or at least outnumbered and outvoted, when all the facts have been laid out. Of course, if you merely outvote them, you'll still have to prove that chickens can be good neighbors by making sure they don't become a nuisance.

Many people *do* like and appreciate chickens, and with proper education and support, laws can be changed. You might enlist support from backyarders in nearby towns where there have been no problems. Some groups are eager to help change discriminating chicken laws. One not-to-be-missed website is www.madcitychickens.com/. Madison, Wisconsin, is known as Mad City for more than one reason, and their "poultry underground" is a good example. The *Mad City Chickens* DVD (Tarazod Films) is worth watching, and an excellent public relations tool for a public showing.

> **Cacklings**
>
> Regulations allowing chickens usually come with certain restrictions, such as numbers, coop size, and setback from property lines and homes. The City of West Torrens, Australia, goes a bit further. Laying hens are allowed, but chicken coops must be painted *green!*

In the final analysis, it all comes down to public relations. Nobody but an irrational grouch could complain about chickens that don't even make their presence known (although such grouches abound). But even an avowed chicken lover—maybe *especially* a chicken lover—would not put up with a flock of noisy, smelly birds in an unsanitary and unsightly setting.

Maybe spending a few extra bucks on an attractive coop isn't such a bad idea after all.

> **Cocktail Conversation**
>
> It has become common for people to share their homes and gardens through home tours and garden strolls. So it's not surprising that some are showing off their chicken coops as well. Many towns and cities have "tours des coops," which help educate urbanites about backyard poultry. Like open people houses, these are great for getting new ideas.

Chickens and Gardeners

Chickens and gardens go together like ham and eggs. People who want to grow at least some of their own food can easily produce both vegetables and eggs, even in a small space. Yes, unrestricted, chickens will destroy both vegetables and flowers with wild abandon. Compare them to fire, which can be destructive and deadly if it gets out of hand, but valuable if it's properly harnessed and controlled.

Even if you live on a very small lot and only have one or two chickens, you probably have a few grass clippings, and certainly some weeds, along with table scraps that can be recycled in the chicken coop. And the manure from one or two birds can easily be worked into a small garden area where it will decompose naturally and inoffensively.

With more space, and perhaps a vegetable plot, the possibilities increase enormously. Gardens must be weeded and often thinned. Vegetable gardens always have damaged or surplus produce that chickens will relish. What you call "waste" or trimmings, the chickens will call dinner. With more garden space you can feed more chickens, and also utilize more manure. Just be sure not to give the chickens more than they will clean up in a short time (maybe an hour), and *never* allow feed to heat up or become moldy.

Cacklings

Fresh chicken manure averages 1.6 percent N (nitrogen), 1.5 P (phosphorus), and 0.9 K (potassium). These values vary with age, feed, moisture content, and the book you find them in, but actually they're pretty meaningless anyway. An organic fertilizer such as manure or compost contains much more than a bag of synthetic fertilizer with the same N-P-K numbers, including that all-important organic matter. All things considered, chicken manure is among the best of fertilizers.

Chicken manure is a "hot" manure; in its fresh state it can burn plants because of its nitrogen content. If you work it into the soil, don't plant anything there for at least a month. On the other hand, the nitrogen makes it excellent for composting with high carbon materials such as dry leaves.

Recycling with Chickens

Some people have suggested that urban chickens could ease pressure on landfills by recycling table scraps and food waste. I find that reasoning hard to follow, considering that table scraps can be composted as easily as manure, and with less effort. However, the two certainly are connected, and if one chicken will convert 7 to 9 pounds of food waste per month to eggs and manure, it's certainly a winning situation. But you'll still need a compost bin, or pile. Compost bins are now available in a wide array of sizes, styles, colors, and prices, and building one yourself is simple.

Cacklings

For years, I have been using a piece of wire fencing 3 feet high and about 9 feet long, made into a cylinder with one end attached to the other by simply bending the wires. All of our compostables go into the bin. When one is full, start another one. When the compost is finished, or if it needs turning, merely untwist the wires, remove the fencing, and you have a neat cylindrical stack.

Everybody should be involved in composting, whether they garden, have chickens, or not: it's the only logical way to deal with organic waste. If you don't garden, you certainly know someone who does and who would be overjoyed to take finished compost off your hands. A gardener can never have too much compost! If you're already recycling yard and kitchen waste, adding that from the poultry yard isn't a big deal. (Note that cat and dog manure should not be composted because of possible pathogens. Chicken manure is okay. Another reason why chickens are better city pets than cats or dogs!)

While instructions on composting are beyond the scope of this book, keep in mind that composting saves valuable landfill space and recycles nutrients instead of burying them in airless pits where they only create methane, a significant greenhouse gas. Putting "waste" through a garbage disposal only increases the burden on sewage treatment plants, which increases your taxes and stresses water resources. You can now purchase electric composters that can be used even in an apartment kitchen. Composting makes sense for everybody, whether they raise chickens or not. For chicken raisers, I consider it a necessity. (For more information on composting, see *The Complete Idiot's Guide to Self-Sufficient Living*.)

Cacklings

Get a book about vermicomposting, such as *Worms Eat My Garbage* by Mary Applehof. It's a good way to recycle what chickens won't eat, most notably coffee grounds and filters, tea bags, and even shredded paper. After the worms multiply, instead of going fishing, feed them to the chickens. The leftover worm bedding, called castings, is even better than compost for gardens.

The Least You Need to Know

- Three types of people generally protest the raising of chickens in towns or cities: those with alektorophobia (fear of chickens); those who believe in separation of town and country; and those with legitimate sanitation and noise concerns.

- Regulations governing chickens in towns and cities vary widely across the country.

- Illegal avians are not uncommon. In fact, the underground approach to poultry raising in towns and cities is more common than you might think.

- Chicken manure is great fertilizer, but it must be composted to avoid burning plants.

Chapter 10

The Social Scene

In This Chapter

◆ Birds of a feather flock together

◆ Elementary education

◆ Poultry clubs and associations

◆ Take a chicken vacation

For the most part, raising chickens is a solitary activity: it's just you and your birds. Some people like it that way. In fact, a friend once told me, "The more I see of people, the better I like chickens."

And yet, when chicken lovers get together, look out! Turns out they enjoy flocking together as much as their birds do. Here are some of the ways you can join them.

How It Started

There has been a social side to chicken raising since the very beginning. Domestication of *Gallus gallus* originated with cockfighting, and there wouldn't be any point in a cockfight with only one spectator. Usually, there were many, sometimes in cockpits built like amphitheaters, with rows of seats rising up from the center. In many cultures, the cockfight was the highlight of social interaction—and in some, it still is. And this is without counting the illegal and therefore clandestine fights that still take place today, according to people who have seen them. (Oklahoma banned cockfighting in 2002; New Mexico in 2007; and Louisiana in 2008. Being illegal doesn't necessarily mean being nonexistent.)

Cocktail Conversation

I suggested that cockfights might still be held in some places where they have been traditional, but how could I prove it? Then I took a break and scanned the day's mail. My attention was immediately drawn to a newspaper headline that read, "Alleged cockfights result in 13 charges" in Madison, Wisconsin!

The modern era of the chicken social scene originated in Europe and spread to North America in the mid-1800s, spurred on in part by the introduction of exotic new breeds from the Far East. A small group of fanciers, mostly well-to-do gentlemen who had been competing among themselves to have the "best" of the new fowls, organized the first American poultry show, held in Boston in 1847. As interest and enthusiasm swelled, the venue was changed from Quincy Market to the more spacious Boston Public Gardens, and it was said that 10,000 spectators showed up. That was the beginning of the six-year-long "Hen Fever," when some people reportedly paid more than $50 for a single chicken. (According to the calculator on the Measuring Worth website, $50 in 1850 would be equivalent to $1,422.08 in 2008.) Fortunes were made, and lost, in chickens.

In February of 1895, *The New York Times* reported "intense interest in the feathered exhibits which characterizes the true fancier," a phenomenon we can witness even today. Also present was "the methodical man, who notes the peculiarities of every bird and commits his catalogue to memory." However, gone are the "daintily-gowned women, with their escorts in evening dress, engaged in animated conversation with the rustic fanciers from Hackensack and other districts." Or maybe not. Back then, Queen Victoria was a well-known chicken raiser. Today, it's Martha Stewart.

As late as 1900, *The New York Times* carried an account of the eleventh annual New York Poultry and Pigeon Association show, with 4,000 birds assembled at Madison Square Garden. The exhibit that attracted the most attention was the black-breasted black game bantams, with the principal winners being "Francis P. Magoun, the banker," and Henry O. Havermeyer Jr. and brother T.A., heirs to a sugar fortune.

The largest exhibitor was Fisher's Island Farm, with 67 entries, including a champion Plymouth Rock, "White Cloud," reportedly a $2,000 bird. There was big money in chickens in those days.

The first show, in 1847, was also the beginning of the American Poultry Association, the oldest livestock organization in the country, although chickens weren't considered "livestock" at that time. The APA covered all recognized breeds, but those who pre-ferred Brahmas or Dorkings, Crevecours or Polish, exclusively, soon banded together just like their respective breeds tend to do when pastured together. There are many such clubs and associations today, and fanciers belong as much (or more) for the social aspects as for the "professional" benefits.

Boys' and Girls' Poultry Clubs

By 1914, the "hen fever" had abated, *The Dollar Hen* (the title of a book written about that time) had taken over, and the more practical side of poultry was in vogue. In February of that year, *The New York Times* reported that "In order to teach the value and importance of the poultry industry, the marketing of products, and the caring for poultry and eggs the Animal Husbandry Division of the Bureau of Animal Industry of the Agricultural Department advocates the forming of boys' and girls' poultry clubs."

4-H

Actually, farm and home "clubs" had been in existence since the 1850s, and 4-H can trace its roots (without the name) to 1902. Some were like correspondence courses, while others were simply corn-growing contests. But the 1914 passage of the Smith-Lever Act put 4-H in the limelight. Club meetings and projects were required.

Many states claim that 4-H poultry projects are among the most popular programs offered. Project areas (for youth 9 to 18 years old) include embryology, raising and rearing poul-try, and poultry and egg consumer projects. In Pennsylvania alone, more than 40,000 students have been enrolled in the poultry program each year since 2000.

> **Cocktail Conversation**
>
> Until 1911, 4-H was 3-H, with a three-leaf clover emblem. In that year "head, heart, and hands" were joined by "health," along with the fourth leaf.

4-H'er Heather Peterson, 11, has been raising and showing poultry in Reno, Nevada, for more than four years. Her favorite is Dark Vader, a Light Brahma, who has been handled since he was a chick and now weighs nearly 14 pounds.

(Photo: Julie Peterson, Reno, Nevada)

Poultry projects go well beyond raising chickens. There are poultry and egg cookery presentation contests, showing, judging contests, quiz bowls, and other events. There are a variety of educational events as well as team and individual competitions. Competitions are held at the county, district, state, and national levels. All of this is also meant to enhance decision-making, communication, and interpersonal skills. Of course, it's also fun—along with awards, prizes, trips, and even college scholarships.

At 4-H events you can even win ribbons with eggs!

(Photo: Jennifer Ortman, Somerset, Ohio)

FFA

The National FFA organization, formerly Future Farmers of America, is more agri-business oriented, although the 1988 name change reflects increased interest in nonproduction areas of agriculture, such as science and business. The poultry slant is decidedly more inclined toward factory farming rather than backyard farming, but still, it's a social as well as educational forum for youth interested in poultry.

Judging eggs, live birds, and carcasses are all considered important. To this end, there are such study aids as flash cards with pictures of chickens' feet, which are examined when evaluating live birds.

Cacklings

One website makes the following suggestion for the FFA egg candling contest, "If you can remember three things you will do well: If the air cell is smaller than a dime, the egg is grade AA; any air cell bigger than a quarter is Grade B; anything in-between is Grade A."

Poultry Science Clubs

Many colleges have poultry science clubs. The one at the University of Wisconsin-Madison has been active since the 1930s. Any student interested in poultry is welcome. Monthly meetings usually include a meal, and activities include a Christmas party and spring barbeque and trips to Atlanta (International Poultry Expo each January) and St. Paul (Midwest Poultry Convention in March). Funds are raised by processing and selling turkeys at Thanksgiving and poultry products in the spring.

Poultry Associations

Breed clubs have no age limits, and many encourage youth participation. The APA/ABA (American Poultry Association/American Bantam Association) Youth Program (www.apa-abayouthprogramsite.org) members must be five or older, with the recommendation that members be able to read and write in order to be tested for level points.

The main objective, as stated on the website, is to help and encourage young people to acquire the knowledge, skills, and experience needed to participate in the poultry fancy as an adult. (Believe me, if you're an adult just starting out, watch out for these kids! Some of them will amaze you.) Like the other youth-oriented poultry programs, this one "promotes opportunities to practice showmanship, cooperation and fellowship and to be involved with their home community and with the poultry fancy in general." The program also "challenges the youth to study, engage in constructive activities, use his/her imagination and to develop individual talents and abilities."

American Poultry Association

The APA itself is geared toward exhibition poultry and shows (www.amerpoultryassn. com). It sanctions shows across the United States and Canada, including an annual national meet. The *American Standard of Perfection*, the last word on exhibition poultry standards, is updated and published by the APA. The American Bantam Association (ABA) plays a similar role with the smaller birds.

A large poultry show, like the Ohio National, is an excellent place to see the best examples of many different breeds in one place, and to talk to the people who breed and exhibit them.

(Photo: Sheri Markley, courtesy of the Ohio National Poultry Show)

> **Cocktail Conversation**
>
> The Wisconsin International Poultry Show (held in Portage), "one of America's prestige poultry shows" and sponsored by the Wisconsin International Poultry Club, invites you to an annual weekend of "fun, fellowship and feathers."

The more laid-back, utilitarian emphasis of most new small flock owners probably keeps these purebred/ showroom organizations from enjoying the growth you might expect in the current chicken boom, but any chicken person will certainly enjoy, and benefit from, attending a good poultry show. Some recent exhibits have hosted 11,000 to 12,000 birds. If you have the opportunity to see thousands of birds of every imaginable breed all in one place, be sure you take advantage of it!

Most shows are much smaller, of course. But even if the shows put on by your local poultry club or county fair are small, the beginner especially should check them out. This is an obvious necessity if you intend to show birds yourself, or if you get involved unintentionally, which has been known to happen. Watching the pros and the judging, studying the chickens and the coop tags, asking questions, and just plain talking and listening are all part of the learning process, and the fun.

Breed Clubs

If you are deeply interested in a particular breed, chances are someone else is, too—and there's a club for it. Just as some breeds are more popular than others, some clubs are bigger and livelier than the rest. If the one you choose to join is a bit on the lean side, maybe you're the one to pep it up. In any case, joining a club and then sitting on the sidelines isn't much fun. The whole point is to get involved, to get in on the action. To get started, see www.feathersite.com/Poultry/BRKBreedClubs.html and www.poultryhelp.com/link-breedclubs.html.

National Poultry Museum

The National Agricultural Center and Hall of Fame was issued a federal charter in 1960. Its mission was to educate society on the historical and present value of American agriculture. It wasn't until 1994 that the first tribute to chickens—the Hatchery Building—was dedicated at the center in Bonner Springs, Kansas. It took another 15 years before the opening of the National Poultry Museum in May 2009. Most of the credit rightfully goes to one man: Loyl Stromberg.

In 1993, Stromberg, then 78, decided to establish a national poultry museum. He was well-known as the author of 14 books on poultry and the founder of Stromberg's Chicks and Pets Unlimited. He was 7 when his parents started a hatchery in 1921, and after graduating in 1932, took over a newly opened Minneapolis branch.

I personally knew Loyl, and wrote about him in *Countryside* magazine. He was the most untiring poultry promoter I have ever met. He was the spark behind the Society for the Preservation of Poultry Antiquities, the catalyst for a number of European poultry tours, and the chief fund-raiser and artifact-finder of the National Poultry Museum. Much of what's on display came from the Stromberg family.

Loyl, in his 90s, was at the 2009 dedication. His long-time dream fulfilled, he received a standing ovation. Today, a visit to the museum is even more interesting and educational than it was in 1994.

Living History Museums

Most Living History Farms feature at least one old breed of poultry, including Sturbridge Village, Colonial Williamsburg, and many less-well-known sites. Garfield Farm Museum, west of Geneva, Illinois, hosts an annual rare breeds show and sale, as well as maintaining a flock of heritage poultry. Check out their yearly calendar at www.garfieldfarm.org/index.html.

To find a living history museum near you, see the Association for Living History Farm and Agricultural Museums (ALHFAM) website at www.alhfam.org.

Coop Tours

There were 18 coops in Austin's first Funky Chicken Coop Tour, held in April 2009, but this was by no means the first in the nation. Raleigh, North Carolina, started their annual open house in 2006, and you can see coops in Madison, Wisconsin; Portland, Oregon; and other locations.

Madison deserves special mention not only for its prominence in the urban chicken movement, but for its lively social scene. Their latest "Pro-Poultry People Potluck Party" was billed as a chance for folks to meet other chicken folks and to talk about different breeds, share photos of coops and chickens, share ideas regarding winter care, find others who would like to be part of an order from a hatchery, and possibly find a reliable "chicken sitter" when you need a few days off. Chicken people are indeed birds of a feather who flock together!

Foreign Tours

If strolling around chicken coops in your hometown or looking at thousands of chickens at national shows isn't enough for you, consider visiting some of the legendary shows of Europe. Fancy poultry has long been more popular there than on this side of the pond. The birds are worth seeing, and the fanciers are worth talking to.

The Organization of German Fancy Fowl Breeders consists of 3 national fancy fowl organizations, 6 regional associations, and 83 "special societies" (breed clubs). A huge show is held in Leipzig every December.

The Poultry Club, active in Britain since 1877, calls itself the world's biggest poultry club. Their National Championship Show, usually held in December at Stoneleigh, is "one of the most prestigious exhibitions in the world." It attracts as many as 6,000 entries, of every conceivable breed.

The Netherlands Poultry Museum (which inspired Loyl Stromberg's dream of opening an American version) is located in Barneveld. It is well known for its poultry and eggs and for being the home of the Barnevelder breed of chicken.

In the past there have been organized tours, allowing Americans to get VIP treatment at the shows and private showings of some of the top breeders' flocks and facilities. No doubt someone will pick up on this again.

Meanwhile, The International Center for Poultry has been sponsoring Australia/New Zealand poultry tours since 2006, with participants visiting local breeders as well as a major show (http://centerforpoultry.org/?page_id=2). Their tours are in the summer—which of course is winter down under, meaning the birds are in their finest condition.

A Lifelong Hobby

So whether you're 5 or 95, chickens and poultry people can be a part of your social life. Just get out and scratch around a bit and you'll find new ideas, new friends, and new ways to enjoy poultry as a fascinating, lifelong hobby.

The Least You Need to Know

- There are poultry programs for children as young as five.
- FFA and 4-H programs educate youth in several areas of poultry science, as well as personal development.
- There are national, local, and breed clubs to meet all your needs for poultry information and fellowship.
- True poultry enthusiasts spend their vacations attending poultry shows, at home and abroad.

Raising Chickens "Organically"

In This Chapter

- ◆ Are your eggs organic?
- ◆ What is free-range?
- ◆ Feeding your chickens organically
- ◆ Commonsense conclusions

Circumstantial evidence suggests that one reason for today's heightened interest in backyard poultry is organic eggs. But what does "organic" really mean, how important is it, what's involved, and how can you produce your own organic eggs?

The "Organic" Buzzword

"Organic" eggs are one of the fastest-growing segments of the food industry. But what does "organic" mean? Unfortunately, not much.

From the beginning of the organic farming movement, the word, and the practices, have been controversial. When the U.S. Department of

Agriculture issued standards for anyone using the official "organic" label in 2000 (after many years of debate), it was a sign that organic farming had arrived, but it was also a signal to many other producers that organic farming was here to stay and that they needed to get involved in order to maximize profits. And with the official standards set forth by the USDA, it's easy to maximize profits by cutting corners (as we'll see).

But why and how did the organic model emerge? What's wrong with the regular eggs that are produced so cheaply in such large numbers?

The Miserable Life of a Caged Hen

Most people today are aware of the cramped spaces allotted to the birds that provide their eggs. Industry standards allow as little as 67 square inches per bird, and not all egg producers comply. (The page you're reading is about 63 square inches. Imagine a chicken *living* on this page.) Nearly as many have probably heard of even more horrible aspects of aptly named egg factories.

Drug-Laden Chicken Feed

The caged hen's miserable life includes feed. After someone hears about laying hens being fed feather meal, chicken litter, and animal byproducts including "spent hen meal" (ground-up dead chickens), no wonder they crave organic eggs!

> **Fox Alert**
>
> Egg cartons that proclaim "No Hormones" are nothing but bluff to make you think you're getting something better than the average: hormone products are not used in any egg production, so the claim is meaningless.

Antibiotics are a big issue. The Food and Drug Administration doesn't allow routine use of antibiotics in poultry, but "routine use" seems to be a hazy term.

As with the "No Hormones" claim, many other claims, including those describing so-called "organic" eggs, are meaningless.

Decoding the "Organic" Buzz

It's true that any product with the "USDA organic" emblem must meet certain standards:

♦ Birds must be cage-free and given outdoor access.

♦ Birds cannot be given antibiotics even if they get sick.

◆ Chicken feed must be free from animal byproducts and grown without chemical pesticides, fertilizers, irradiation, genetic engineering, or sewage sludge.

Other standards exist as well; some are set by local organizations. But are those standards high enough, and does every producer follow them? How are they enforced? Let's look at some of these concerns.

Cage Free?

The term *cage free* sounds good, but all the Department of Agriculture requires of this claim is that the chickens don't live in cages. They can still live without ever seeing the sun or breathing fresh air, and in crowded conditions.

Free range is a step up, because now the cage-free chickens must have access to the outdoors—unless a health risk is present. But define "access." Define "health risk." Who's to question the producer who keeps his chickens inside because he thinks West Nile Disease from mosquitoes, or avian flu from wild birds, or winter weather, are health risks? In addition, "outdoors" could mean a blacktopped parking lot, no matter how small, with no access to forage. The USDA regulates the term "free range" with poultry meat, but not eggs.

Pasture-raised would seem to imply chickens living by foraging on pasture. The term is not regulated, however, and should be taken with a grain of salt.

Natural is meaningless except on meat, where the label prohibits such additives as artificial ingredients including flavoring, coloring, and chemical preservatives. Eggs are natural, naturally.

There is nothing wrong with any of these words, or the practices they imply. What's wrong is that too many egg producers fudge on the terms and the methods. People who know and care little about the spirit of organic farming have jumped on the bandwagon because that's where the money is. Not incidentally, that's also where the future lies, but we're not there yet.

Antibiotics in Feed

Antibiotics have been added to feed at low levels to promote growth by suppressing minor problems. The rise of antibiotic-resistant infections in people—and particularly after 9/11, the fear of terrorist-launched anthrax that would be resistant to antibiotics—resulted in a public outcry that the largest poultry producers, including Tyson, and sellers, such as McDonald's, couldn't ignore. By 2002, antibiotic feed additives were being quietly discontinued.

The change was helped by a 2007 study by Johns Hopkins Bloomsberg School of Public Health researchers concluding that feeding antibiotics was not cost effective. In fact, use of the additives resulted in a loss of $0.0093 per chicken. Applied to the roughly 10 billion broilers slaughtered annually, that ain't chicken feed.

Still, the report claimed that even without Tyson, two-thirds of the chickens being grown for meat continued getting the additives at the time of the study.

Arsenic in Feed

Arsenic (in the form of Roxarsone) is added to feed in small amounts to kill parasites and promote growth. It was approved in the United States in the 1960s. The European Union conducted tests and immediately banned arsenic in chicken feed in the 1980s. In 2004, a similar study in the United States reached similar conclusions, but a spokesman for the National Chicken Council disagreed, saying the study was "much ado about nothing." Tyson Foods discontinued the use of arsenic that year, but others continue the practice.

Arsenic is present in other foods, notably rice. It's found in soil and water. One of the main problems is that since adding it to chicken feed was first approved in the 1960s, consumption of chicken has increased dramatically, and the ingestion of arsenic along with it. We're exposed to a lot more of it than we were 40 or 50 years ago.

> **Cacklings**
>
> Only a few years ago it was all but impossible to find organic chicken feed. The laws of supply and demand are working, and organic feed is becoming more available all the time. However, expect to pay about twice as much for it. For the latest scoop on who's selling it in your area, check these websites: www.henspa.com/store/ccp0-catshow/deed.html and www.lionsgrip.com/producers.html.

Why do poultry producers use all this stuff? Mostly because when 10,000 to 100,000 birds are in one house, one sick bird can mean disaster. You don't medicate just one bird out of thousands. With chickens so closely confined and packed together, even a slight problem could wipe out the entire flock, literally overnight. In fact, this was common in the early days of confinement housing, before antibiotics were used. An ounce of prevention is certainly worth more than a pound of cure.

However, many thinking people consider mass medication equal to putting a Band-Aid on a cancer. It doesn't address the real cause of the problem, which is the confinement system. Anyone with a small flock who has close daily contact with each individual has no use, or need, for these chemicals. With proper management, those ideals can be applied to larger, commercially viable flocks. This kind of management is happening.

Determining Nutritional Standards for Your Backyard Flock

If you want organic eggs, you must raise your chickens according to organic practices, especially with regard to what you feed them. To make any sense of sound nutritional practices, however, it's best to set aside any preconceived notions about organics and start from the beginning. What does a chicken actually need to survive and prosper? After that it will be much easier to revisit your feeding options.

At the beginning of the twentieth century, little thought was given to chicken feed. One reason was that very little was known about nutrition of any kind. Besides, chickens foraged for most of their food, which the farm wife supplemented with kitchen scraps and perhaps a bit of grain snitched from the more "valuable" animals. And don't forget: chicken dinners were rare, usually reserved for special guests; and few people ate eggs in winter.

Then came several massive changes, rapidly and almost simultaneously. Just as chickens were starting to move from the freedom of the open barnyard to large poultry houses, the first vitamin was discovered (McCollum and Davis, vitamin A, 1912–1914). New discoveries and ideas followed at a furious pace. Geneticists developed new strains of chickens for maximum egg or meat production; the introduction of electricity helped bring about artificial incubation and lighting, as well as automated feeding and watering; and chicken nutrition was honed into a science.

If we want to break it down into groaning detail, we could note that chickens require more than 40 chemical compounds or chemical elements to support life, growth, and reproduction. In most cases, scientists learned about these elements by leaving them out of a diet, one at a time, and observing what happened. Arginine deficiency in chicks results in poor feathering and subnormal growth. Vitamin D deficiency in chicks causes rickets; in hens, weak eggshells, and then no eggs at all. Eliminate vitamin E, and you'll have chicks with encephalomalacia, a nervous syndrome involving ataxia (involuntary muscle movements) that kills chicks, usually from 15 to 30 days old. All 40 elements are essential.

Looking into Scientifically Balanced Rations

Now let's return to the large-scale poultry producer. Where are chickens kept inside going to get their required nutrients? Certainly not from corn, which contains only a few, and not from any other grain or combination of grains, which are likewise deficient. A scientifically balanced ration requires ingredients from many sources, which might include blood meal, distillers' dried solubles (today, often a byproduct of ethanol production), animal tallow and lard, hydrolyzed poultry feathers, poultry byproduct meal, dried whey, dried brewer's yeast, and fish meal, along with such standards as bone meal and alfalfa and soybean meal.

Now, your mission—should you choose to accept it—is to combine as many of these ingredients as necessary, in the proper proportions, to keep your chickens healthy, happy, and productive. Just think about finding these ingredients in small quantities, grinding or preparing and mixing them, and you will understand why I advise patronizing the nearest feed store, organic or not.

Chickens spend most of their time foraging. Sometimes that's tough.

(Photo: Delia Daba, Kenosha, Wisconsin)

Organics Is More Than Just Feed

The real question of organic food is not whether there might be a tiny bit of feather meal in the chicken feed and infinitely less in the egg, but whether the chicken was treated humanely and had at least *some* access to natural foods.

Organics involves an entire philosophy of farming and a way of living, not just the manner in which you feed an animal. The overall effects of any particular food on soil, water, people, or the entire ecosystem, are much more important than any specific detail. In my view, by raising chickens to produce your own eggs, you have taken a much greater step toward organic eating and living than someone who merely worries about whether the eggs she buys are certified organic. Feed is only a small part of it.

Now I certainly don't mean to imply that there is no such thing as an honestly organic egg in a supermarket. Hundreds of honest, dedicated, extremely knowledgeable people are producing and selling truly organic eggs (and meat). Joel Salatin, a pioneer and proficient promoter of pastured poultry products, has many followers and even more admirers. His is certainly the way of the future for commercial producers.

I also know smaller operators who prepare their own organic chicken feed and are very successful. Harvey Ussery is a prime example, and you can learn about his methods at www. themodernhomesteader.us.

> **Cocktail Conversation**
>
> Think of what chickens eat scratching in barnyard manure, and maybe feather meal won't seem so bad. Besides, feathers are being used in some other applications you probably don't want to know about. Remember what we just learned about keratin, nature's all-purpose plastic? Some people think keratin would make great capsules—the kind medicine comes in.

Mass Production vs. the Backyard Model of Production

The technicians whose primary stated goal is producing food at minimum cost (and maximum profit), with little or no regard for true value and quality, often say it would be impossible to feed the world without their mass production methods. They contend that backyarders and homesteaders are only playing at food production.

This is obviously true for some people with a few pet-type chickens, but it is false as a blanket indictment. During World War II, more than 40 percent of the vegetables consumed in America came from backyard Victory Gardens. That situation could easily happen again, and eggs could be included as part of the food production. Backyarders could not produce their product as cheaply as mass producers, but it would be more valuable and sustainable. For a more detailed discussion of this aspect of home food production, see my most recent book, *The Complete Idiot's Guide to Self-Sufficient Living*.

Mass-produced food, including poultry products, is cheap—but at what price? There's no argument that we're saving a few cents with modern production methods, but what are those methods costing us in terms of health and social and environmental degradation?

Cocktail Conversation

It's an old saying that "Water is the most important feed." A chicken's body is 55 to 75 percent water, depending on age, with young birds containing more. An egg is about 65 percent water. And of course, water carries nutrients—it's essential for metabolic reactions and for waste elimination, as well as helping to maintain body temperature. Never let your chickens run out of water.

The alternative is small-scale, *truly* organic production, including backyard farms. Even using commercial feeds with their hydrolyzed feathers and other ingredients, such a system is vastly more "organic" and sustainable than the industrial agribusiness model. Without those commercial feeds, backyarding could well be impossible for many. Organic feeds are becoming more common and will continue to become more available as demand increases. But we have to start someplace, and the ratchet effect can be very effective. The only possible place to start is where you are now, and for most backyard poultry raisers, that means using commercial feed (organic or not).

I hope I have made my point. I have used a lot of words in the attempt, because very few people understand all the nuances of organic food production, and it's important information. But let's get back to feeding chickens, organically or not.

Life Stages: Yet Another Variable to Consider

By now it should be easier to see why, when we were talking about starting out with chicks in Chapter 3, I said you'd need three different types of feed: a starter ration, formulated for the special needs of young developing chicks; then a grower ration; and finally a feed that satisfies the requirements of the laying hen. Needing three types of feed complicates matters, because if you want to create your own chicken feed, you have to mix three different kinds at three different stages. For the smallholder, mixing even one feed is problematic, for several reasons.

The chief ingredient in poultry feed is grain. But cereal grains are low in protein, which must be provided from other sources. What's more, proteins are made of about 20 different amino acids, most of which are essential. (Nonessential amino acids can be synthesized by the body, so they're nonessential only in the sense that they don't have to be added to the feed.) Various feed ingredients have various levels of amino acids, and this too has to be carefully balanced out, often in the interest of low-cost feed. In addition, some nutrients are required in such tiny quantities that it would be impossible to purchase them economically, and just as difficult to properly mix them into the ration.

Virtually all commercial poultry foods are about 60 percent corn, milo (grain sorghum), or wheat, and 25 to 30 percent soybean meal. The other ingredients are minor in volume, but not in importance.

The primary adjustment made for age involves protein. Young, growing birds and animals need more. Since protein is the most expensive major nutrient, and any excess is wasted, it makes sense to match the feed to the needs of the bird. A young chick needs more protein than an older one, and a laying hen needs the least. It won't harm the laying hen to get more; it will just cost more.

Conversely, a pullet only needs 1 percent calcium. A laying hen requires about 3.5 percent, or she will be forced to pull calcium from her bones to make eggshells, which is obviously not good.

Scratch Feed: An Incomplete Ration

By now it should also be obvious that scratch feed, consisting entirely of grains, is not a complete ration. This is what Grandma scattered in the yard for her hens. A hundred years ago she probably thought she was "feeding" them, in the sense of providing nutrition. In reality, she was mostly giving them something to do, and keeping them near the house to make egg-gathering and protection easier.

The same can be said for kitchen and garden waste. Yes, chickens are omnivores, like humans. That doesn't mean their nutritional needs are identical, and it doesn't suggest that those needs will be met with food scraps. Waste and trimmings must be treated like scratch feed, not a complete ration.

But now we have come full circle and can connect the dots. Scratch, or any grain-based feed, can provide the energy birds need *if they have access to natural foods containing the other essential elements required for good nutrition.* If you have enough suitable land, and the birds can be adequately protected, you are well on the way to producing truly organic eggs. Egg production on this level is not a viable economic model because of pesky details like winter, which results in both the lack of suitable forage and decreasing day length. Presumably we do want to continue to eat eggs in winter, and we don't want to pay exorbitant, or even just unnecessary, amounts of money for poultry products.

Chickens enjoy fruits and vegetables, but these foods don't provide all the elements of nutrition they need.

(Photo: Carolyn Buck, Buck Farms, Petaluma, California)

This is where compromise becomes necessary. Industrial agribusiness is coming under pressure on many economic and environmental fronts, just as true organic food production is becoming more viable. The organic system will eventually prevail because it's the only sustainable system. Meanwhile, those caught in the middle have to take the best, or the least objectionable, of both worlds.

Which brings us back to my feeding advice in Chapter 1: Give your birds access to as much natural food as possible, which in most urban and suburban settings won't be nearly enough. Then buy a bag of feed. You might not find an organic feed today, but soon there might not be any other kind.

The Least You Need to Know

◆ Most organic standards don't mean much, and many aren't monitored or enforced.

◆ The need for medicated feed arises from crowded, stressful living conditions.

◆ The need for scientifically balanced feed stems from the inability of mass-produced birds to forage, and the quest for year-round, low-cost meat and eggs.

◆ Eggs from your backyard flock are more organic than many so-called "organic" eggs on the market, even if you don't buy organic feed.

12

Can I Make Money Raising Chickens?

In This Chapter

◆ The profit motive

◆ Options and opportunities

◆ Change is in the wind

◆ Follow the leaders

Sooner or later, even if only for one crazy moment, you are going to pause, gaze upon your chickens with pride, and say, "Gosh, this is fun. And so easy! Twice as many chickens wouldn't be any more work. I wonder … could I make a little money, raising chickens?"

Let's talk about that.

Incremental Growth Is Easy

If you have three or four laying hens, the flock size we've been assuming for much of this book, you might get close to two dozen eggs in a very good week, with some very good layers. Assuming you want a few of those eggs for yourself, you have nothing worth selling. And there's no point in getting people excited about your wonderful eggs, because next week or next month, you might not have any to sell. It's better to give them away, maybe by the handful instead of by the dozen, to neighbors or special friends.

If you live in the countryside and have the room, facilities, time, and interest to raise perhaps a few dozen birds, the situation changes. If you have gained a little experience, are a very good manager, and have a little luck, you might very well build up a small egg trade, most likely among friends, neighbors, relatives, and co-workers. On that scale you won't have to worry about regulations, or even the grading and uniformity most markets require, but naturally you'll want to deliver the best product possible: eggs that are clean, fresh, wholesome, and attractive. This means you will eat those with abnormal shells and other Grade B attributes yourself.

And if you are, or want to become, a real chicken farmer, there are opportunities—in some ways, opportunities that didn't exist only a few years ago. The reasons involve such concepts as cage-free, free-range, and organic.

The Agribusiness Monopoly

A small producer can't possibly compete with the giant egg and broiler companies on price. Big outfits got big because they have been able to shave costs down to absolute minimums, not only on feed and housing, but on everything, including packaging and marketing. They are able to deliver what stores and restaurants want, when they want it, in the quantity they want, and with the uniformity customers demand. They have already jumped through the hoops of any applicable regulations and have all the paperwork in place.

> ### Cocktail Conversation
>
> As of May 1, 2009, 282 million laying hens were in commercial operations in the United States. On that day, according to the USDA, the rate of lay was 72.4 eggs per 100 layers. If you're not going to push for production the way the factory farms do— and that's the whole point, isn't it?—you can't expect even that many eggs on a regular basis.

Of course, they got where they are in part by keeping layers in tiny cages, adding antibiotics to feed, automating everything, and treating chickens as if they were machines in a factory. The result has been poultry products that are unbelievably cheap, huge capital investments, and vertical integration that effectively locks out competition from smaller operators. The result has also been a backlash.

The Organic Challenge

It took many years for "organic" to become anything more than a niche market for long-haired, sandal-wearing, tree-hugging vegetarians, or so it seemed. Those who hadn't been paying attention were probably surprised when, all of a sudden, entire aisles and even sections of their local supermarkets were touting "natural" and "organic" products.

At some point chickens entered the picture. As cages grew smaller, the potential for backlash grew larger. As antibiotic-resistant bugs became more common in hospitals, resistance to antibiotic-fed chickens became more common in supermarkets. At the same time, in a ratchet effect, more and more enterprising organic farmers developed innovative methods to increase production and lower costs, within the organic parameter. They increased production, and the marketing and publicity that accompanied it amplified the backlash. As more people discovered they could actually see and taste the difference, going organic was not just a matter of having pity on the poor chickens or avoiding harmful substances, but a sensible investment in higher-quality food and better living. The new chicken farmers found that they could indeed compete with the giants, not on price, and not on their terms, but on quality, and on organic terms.

A New World Unfolds

This evolution has been happening without any major new developments, discoveries, or government intervention. (The government got involved after the fact. You know the saying from the French Revolution, "There go the people. I must follow them, for I am their leader.") When a cusp point has been reached, the transition from industrial agribusiness back to pure agriculture will continue at an even faster rate. Maybe we have already reached that point.

Effects of Backyard Chickens

As exhibit A, I offer the current interest in backyard and organic poultry, including you and this book. Raising chickens in town might be a fad. I think and hope not, but even if it is, how many people who have now tasted a real egg could go back to the insipid store-bought cage-produced variety? And if their egg experience induced them to try broilers that were produced on pasture, especially from chickens not bred for fast, economical growth, how could they go back to the factory kind?

Considerations like these suggest that the pendulum is swinging back. Efficiency has gone about as far as it can. Now quality is taking over.

New Legislation

Consumers might not even have the opportunity to go back to factory-farmed poultry products. Exhibit B is the new animal welfare law enacted in 2008, in California, of course. The regulations don't go into effect until 2015, and a lot could happen in that time, but the trend is clear.

Proposition 2 decreed that egg-laying hens must be able to stand up, turn around, and stretch their wings without touching another bird or a cage wall. In other words, now that you have read a little about chicken behavior in Chapter 7, you will recognize this as meaning that they must have the opportunity to exercise their chickenness, at least a little.

The rule doesn't mention cage-free housing. But the Humane Society of the United States, which sponsored the measure, admits it was written so no cage systems currently available could meet the requirements. The proposition won by a 63.5 percent landslide, one of the biggest margins ever in a state with a reputation for initiatives. What's more, in 2009 a bill was introduced that would require farmers in other states to meet the same requirements in order to sell eggs in California. Since those producers provide more than half of the 10 billion eggs Californians consume in a year, this is no small potatoes. Since not all of their production goes to California, as California goes, so goes the nation.

500,000 Homeless Hens?

What happens when a farmer with several chicken houses, each the size of a football field and housing 500,000 hens in cages the size of this page, is forced to provide more space for each bird? In a state with a $300 million egg industry, who knows? But the possibilities are fascinating.

One is that costs and egg prices will indeed go up, perhaps to what cage-free eggs cost today. That would make backyard flocks more valuable.

It could also mean that instead of hundreds of thousands of chickens, farmers would raise more manageable (and rational?) numbers, resulting in more but smaller farmers. This has been one of the unheralded goals of organic farmers for more than 50 years!

A snazzy backyard chicken coop like this was unheard of only a few years ago. Now there is a whole cottage industry making and selling a wide variety of small chicken houses. The black trim on this one, from Henspa, is done with Zoopoxy, a long-lasting epoxy finish used in zoos. The white panels are PVC-coated aluminum over 1 inch thick insulation board. The roof is over 1 inch insulation board also. The inside is lined with the same corrugated plastic used in zoo cages and has the same floor as found in commercial chicken settings.

(Photo: Stephen Keel, http://henspa.com)

Combine this development with the already growing backlash against antibiotics, problems with waste disposal, water shortages, and changing lifestyles including unemployment and underemployment as well as simpler living in general, and you have a recipe for significant change. For those who want to eat affordable eggs, backyard chickens could become as common as second cars. In such a scenario, there would be more small family farmers. Some would be very small, and part-time—including those producing food in cities. (Again I refer you to *The Complete Idiot's Guide to Self-Sufficient Living* to fill in the background.)

Options for Your Poultry Business

All of these developments would mean many new opportunities in the poultry—well, maybe we would no longer want to call it an "industry." But if you're serious about poultry as a business, several avenues are open to you right now. For any of them, you will certainly want to gain some experience on a small scale, because it's always wise to learn to walk before you try to run. Knowing what's involved in caring for a few chickens is essential and can serve as a springboard for several money-making options. Here are three examples:

♦ **Eggs:** Selling (free-range) eggs—for "egg money," not to pay off the mortgage—could involve anything from owning a few dozen hens to a few thousand.

♦ **Meat:** Again, free-range and antibiotic-free is a given, but today's Chicken of Tomorrow will also be a slower-growing, less plump breed, with less fat and much more flavor. More on this later in this chapter.

♦ **Live birds:** Already, some enterprising entrepreneurs have stepped up to fill the needs of backyarders looking for their first chickens. They only want (or are allowed) a few, which makes buying from a hatchery difficult; they might want different breeds; and they'd prefer started pullets. The new entrepreneurs buy several hundred chicks of various breeds, coddle them through the brooder stage, and sell them in small lots or even individually as started pullets. Ethnic markets offer other opportunities.

These are the easy, but by no means the only, options and opportunities. Just keep your eyes and mind open. A few years ago it was impossible to buy a small chicken house outside Britain; I don't know how many people are building and selling them today. Maybe you'll come up with an exciting new design for a feeder, or other piece of equipment. At least a few are working on developing new strains, varieties, and even breeds, to meet the new demands. It's a whole new world.

Pastured Poultry

If your interest is egg or meat production, raise a few birds while studying what other successful commercial-size producers are doing. The field is full of innovators and information on their methods. The leading guru, hands down, is Joel Salatin, of Polyface Farm in Swope, Virginia. His 1993 book *Pastured Poultry Profit$* is more than just a classic: it's a bible. He, too, advises starting out by producing no more than your family can consume, until you are certain you can produce a superior product.

Modest Ambitions

Informal surveys of people currently operating small poultry businesses spotlight several interesting points. In no particular order, the poultry is part-time, even for full-time farmers who raise other livestock or crops as well, and few have any desire to get bigger. Nobody's out to displace Tyson. It's easy to sell eggs—up to a point. When you have to reach beyond your circle of friends and co-workers, it's more work and less fun, and not many people will do this kind of work if they don't enjoy it. Eggs are a commodity: the small producer doesn't just walk into a store or restaurant and make a sale. There are occasional success stories in which salesmanship and persistence paid off, but it takes a certain type of person.

Raising broilers (or roasters, or even capons) is easier than selling eggs, in some ways. At least it can be seasonal. Here one of the problems is that the money is in the butchering. You can spend 12 to 16 weeks growing a quality broiler, and then make or lose money at butchering time.

> **Cacklings**
>
> The American Pastured Poultry Producers Association (APPPA) is composed of both meat and egg producers, many of whom have years of experience and a wealth of knowledge. *Raising Poultry on Pasture, Ten Years of Success* is a compilation of articles from the APPPA GRIT newsletter from 1997 to 2005 (www.apppa.org).

Regulations can also get in the way, depending on your location, the scope of your operation, and your visibility.

> **Fox Alert**
>
> With regard to regulations, you can check with various local authorities, but don't expect any straight or accurate answers. One man said three different local officials told him he couldn't slaughter poultry at home. Later, at a seminar, a state official said it was legal to butcher under 1,000. Way fewer restrictions are placed on egg sales than on meat, and they, too, vary widely. You'll have to do your own research, perhaps discreetly. Sometimes it's best just not to ask too many questions.

Keep Genetics in Mind

Raising chickens humanely involves more than housing, feed, and pasture. It starts with the birds themselves. Simply taking what the French call the *industriel* chicken out of its cage and releasing it on pasture doesn't work.

You know something about breeds of chickens now, and you're aware that the hybrids developed for cage laying and for fast and efficient broiler production are not ideal outside the environments they were designed for. For one thing, neither can forage the way a chicken is supposed to. The Cornish crosses are flat-out lazy. Birds developed for economical meat production don't have the flavor and texture of the old breeds, the flavor chicken could and should have. Butchering before the fowl is even mature accentuates that lack. The hapless Cornish cross is prone to leg problems, and many die of heart attacks. They are not happy birds.

The Chicken of Tomorrow Is Outdated

And yet, the old, heirloom breeds don't quite get the job done either. This was recognized even before 1948, when the A&P grocery chain (the first national supermarket) sponsored the "Chicken of Tomorrow" contest. Breeders from across the country competed for a $5,000 prize to develop the broiler that came closest to a broad-breasted model the experts considered the ideal. The birds resulting from that contest helped revolutionize broiler production worldwide, but the "improvements" didn't end there. Intensive genetic selection for rapid growth has placed enormous pressure on these birds. An increased need for oxygen leaves them prone to heart failure and "waterbelly," or ascites. Rapid weight gains impede their ability to walk. Maybe it's not surprising that the Cornish cross is still the meat bird of choice, even among free-range producers, but a growing number of people wonder why.

However, it's not necessary to throw out the baby with the bathwater: the choice is not between heirloom breeds and the unnatural freaks. It would be entirely possible to go back, perhaps to 1948 and the notion of a chicken for a new tomorrow, and develop the best of both worlds through smarter breeding practices. Today's chicken of tomorrow doesn't have to balloon into a flavorless mound of mushy meat with drumsticks within a few weeks, like the 1948 model eventually became. On the other hand, it must be able to survive in a natural environment, without constant medication, foraging for some of its own food, and it must be flavorful.

A number of small flock owners have been breeding for a better chicken for years, without fanfare. Instead of butchering the biggest and best rooster when company comes for Sunday dinner, as was customary, they save the best for breeding stock and cull the others. It's really quite a logical and simple process, although progress can be both slow and spotty for the casual breeder. Most are amateur geneticists, but so were the developers of most of the major old breeds and, of course, the top poultry exhibitors of any era.

The Corndel Breed

One breeder who made notable progress was Tim Shell, who set out with some definite goals in mind. A major one was to develop a new breed—not a hybrid, requiring two different parent lines, but a bird that would breed true so that homesteaders could propagate their own flocks without buying hybrid chicks every year. He crossed Cornish with Delawares, a popular meat breed from the mid-1900s, and named them Corndels. Using line breeding and careful selection, he was able to produce a chicken that breeds true and produces the qualities he wanted without further crossing.

Although he and his family later moved out of the country to preach pastured poultry in China, his flock was dispersed enough that the line is still being maintained and improved through selection. Corndel chickens have a following.

The French Connection

For even more years of even greater success, you'll have to look to France and the *Label Rouge* program.

Of special interest to us, especially in light of the coming changes in California, is how the chickens are raised. For starters, the fast-growing Cornish-crosses that are the mainstay of world broiler production are not allowed: meat quality is paramount, and that means slower growth. These birds reach 5 pounds in 12 weeks, instead of the now-conventional 6 to 7 weeks. Broilers are raised in small houses (400 square meters maximum per house, 4,304 square feet) with a limit of four such houses per farm and at least 2 square meters per bird (22 square feet) of free-range pasture, or about 2 acres per house. Maximum stocking rate is 11 chickens per square meter, or 4,400 for the house. Therefore, the limit is 17,600 per farm, a far cry from the hundreds of thousands on factory farms.

def•i•ni•tion

Label Rouge (Red Label) was started in 1965 by a group of poultry breeders who were anxious to farm according to their traditions, in contrast to the then-new factory methods, and they also wanted to give consumers a quality guarantee. The distinctive red label is now accepted as an official sign of superior quality, on many farm products besides chicken.

Feed must contain at least 75 percent cereals. No animal products, growth stimulants, or other additives are allowed. Fish meal is banned because it might be mistaken for animal byproduct meal. Vaccination and coccidiostats are allowed (see Chapter 8); routine prophylactic medication is not. Neither are beak or toe trimming.

The broilers are slaughtered at 81 to 110 days, when they are twice as old as regular chickens, which improves the flavor and texture. Maximum traveling time to a processor must be less than two hours, or 64 miles, and the carcasses must be air-chilled (a rare process in the United States; more on the importance of air chilling in Chapter 13). Local foods are big in France, and they're becoming important here, too.

Cocktail Conversation

Note that Red Label is not a brand; it's a nationwide blanket seal of approval, with many local brands competing on the basis of *terroir,* a common wine term referring to characteristics a product acquires from the climate, soil, and farming methods of a specific region. The Slow Food Movement, eating locally, and eating seasonally are as much a part of the appeal as are organic methods of farming.

The big chicken lobby in the United States would go bonkers over restrictions like these and would certainly protest that no one would buy such expensive meat. But although *Label Rouge* costs twice as much as *industriel* products, it enjoys 30 percent of the French poultry market.

SASSO Breeds and Varieties

Those *Label Rouge* chickens from France are making the most headway in much of the world, and are just starting to pip in the United States. SASSO was established by *Label Rouge* with the objective of breeding strains capable of producing high-quality poultry that are both full of flavor and cost-effective for producers. SASSO is one of the leading suppliers to the poultry-rich Philippines. Another major producer is Hubbard-ISA. Imagine: a world leader in poultry breeding for more than 85 years, now selling *slow-growing* chickens! You'll have a hard time locating any as of this writing, but keep your eyes open. It is indeed a different world.

The Black Walnut Chicken

Here is a true story that not only illustrates the theme of this chapter, but also ties many parts of this book together and then brings us full circle, back to the opening paragraphs about how our grandparents raised chickens.

Gene McCraw is a homesteader. He lives on a small farm in the Ozarks, where he was raised. After studying agriculture at the University of Arkansas and spending 10 years with Tyson Foods as a technical advisor, this widower and his three teenage daughters milk two cows and make all of their own dairy products, including cave-aged hard cheeses. They raise their own beef and chicken, have a large garden, and supplement their diet with wild foods. And they have developed their own breed of chicken.

A typical Black Walnut hen.

(Photo: The McCraws)

Overcoming the Predator Problem

Gene said the most difficult part of raising chickens in his locale, even when he was growing up, has been the predator problem. "Dogs helped, traps helped, and proximity to the house helped, but the inevitable disappointment from discovering the loss of many or most of the birds has led me to abandon the attempt to keep a predator-proof chicken house, along with the subsequent night-time trips responding to the ruckus. We discovered, by default, a way to overcome this problem."

Surprisingly, he overcame the problem by providing the birds no shelter or protection at all! He still loses some to varmints, but not on the scale of the losses in pens. "Predator problems usually come from having the birds confined in a house, unable to escape, thus allowing large kills rather than just one or two birds. Our dogs also protect the flock, but our worst predator kills have always been in attempting to keep the house predator-tight, which is very difficult." However, these are not just any breed of chicken. Gene and the girls have been developing them over the past eight years.

"We call them Black Walnut chickens, because they are usually black, we live in Walnut Valley, and they are tough as a nut and tasty as a kernel. They have survived snow and ice storms, sub-zero temperatures, they stay out in the rain, and have even been completely knocked out of their roost trees by hail storms. The only disadvantage to this type of production model is the need to cover any newer automobiles that you do not wish to have scratched by their landing on them. Of course, we fence out our garden rather than fence in our chickens." Black birds seem less vulnerable to losses, especially to hawks and owls. This is also true of cats, he noted: "A white cat doesn't survive long here."

Another drawback is harvesting. "We can get one or two at feeding, but they roost too high in the trees to catch them easily at night. Most of our slaughter is by head shot from a .22."

On the other hand, disease and parasite problems don't become concentrated, as they do with a house and yard. While the manure is spread over a wide area, a surprising amount is recovered for garden use because the chickens always roost in the same spot. A hen will have her special place on a specific tree branch to return to every night. The manure builds up under the branches and can be picked up.

Free-Range or Feral?

Their diet is mainly insects and worms and whatever they can forage, supplemented with a small amount of scratch, mainly to keep them tame. "Since they are free to roam, it gives their 'free-range' status much more meaning. We encourage them to lay in provided nest boxes which they utilize fairly well, but we also know to check certain kinds of areas for other nests. This unrestricted living also allows them to break up the cow patties and spread the manure while they eat any grain and fly larvae present."

They are good layers, small but good meat birds; the hens are good mothers; the young stay in the area where they were brooded; they survive in a wild and predator-heavy area; and they endure a rather harsh environment. It sounds like the perfect bird for this particular situation, but it "just happened."

Like many others, the McCraws ignored the old rule about building the chicken house *before* you get the chickens. Gene intended to build a house to enclose the birds at night, despite his past lack of success with that method. "But before we knew it, the birds were thriving by taking care of themselves and winter had arrived." A chicken house became a priority for the next spring, but by then the chickens were increasing in number, without a house!

The McCraws once saved the head of a butchered steer with a nice set of horns by hanging it in a tree to dry. Flies "blew" the head, maggots fell to the ground, and the chickens scarfed them up. And there were many fewer flies around. This gave rise to the "Walnut Fly Abatement Program." They now routinely hang the heads of butchered animals. "It only smells for a few days," Gene says.

(Photo: The McCraws)

The Foundation Stock

The McCraws started with standard heavy breeds such as Rhode Island Reds, but found Black Australorps had the best survival rate. These crossed with mostly black bantams and some game stock from local farms. "Then we just let nature take its course. I would estimate we have a half standard breed, three-eighths bantam, and one-eighth game chicken. Too much game and they range too far and their nests are too concealed. Too much bantam and they and the eggs are too small. Over half conventional-breed genetics and they lack the sense of survival and hardiness we need."

At first they tried to select for coloring they thought was pretty. The roosters had something to say about that. "Once two roosters have decided to fight, unless you intervene to settle the argument by killing one, they will do it themselves sooner or later. I suppose this is the game and bantam blood tendencies. Incidentally, our roosters have never shown any sign of aggression towards us, as contrasted with many domestics confined to a house or yard where they become more territorial and hence meaner. Setting hens are another matter: leave the hens alone once they have chicks!"

Now, the 150 or so hens are divided into several smaller flocks, led by the roosters that control that "district." When the teenaged roosters become too annoying, it's time to put a dozen or so in the freezer.

"The population is controlled by how many eggs we allow the hens to brood. You can't stop these hens from setting, but you can take their eggs away. Sometimes we miss a nest and a hen will emerge with 10 or so new chicks to surprise us. We always have more eggs than we can eat, so we sell some, and use some cooked eggs for dog food, etc."

No Record Keeping

With such a system, he obviously couldn't tell me how many eggs a hen lays, but he does know that hens five, and even eight years old, are still laying and setting. "They don't lay all year individually, but some are always laying, so we always have eggs. Molt, for whatever reason, is not noticeable, and they seem to slow down over a long period rather than stop laying abruptly. The staggered nature of their laying cycles, while favoring spring and summer, seems less dependent on day length and more on temperature. We have had some hens setting during the winter. Of course, we haven't had severe winters now for several years."

The meat is described as being "very good," but of a "substantially different texture" than that of confined chickens. It's not "watery tender," like the factory-raised broilers. Gene said, "Eight weeks of feeding started chicks (three weeks old) should produce a broiler around four pounds live weight." That's about the weight of the hens. "We are great advocates of slow cooking, and these birds are superb in a crock pot as whole chickens." He thinks the meat and eggs from these chickens are far superior to those coming from other methods of production. The meat has concentrated flavor, and the eggs, with their bright orange yokes, are truly gourmet.

Not for Everyone, But ...

Gene knows this production model will not work for everyone, or in every situation. "A population of approximately 200 fits our six-acre spot (and surrounding woods) without taking too much toll on the other farm enterprises. More than this would tend to leave too much bare ground from scratching. We want enough chickens to eat all the bugs, scatter all the manure, survive the threats, supply us, and leave all the grass sod."

The maintenance-free Black Walnuts keep the McCraws in eggs and meat year-round, with a surplus to sell. Until recently, their self-sufficient model was aimed at providing all of their own food, without marketing any excess. This has been changing as of late, Gene said. "Now, by taking more of the excess fertile eggs and selling or incubating them, we might sell some of this 'breed' to others with this kind of farm." He hopes to have a web page in the near future and can be contacted at walnutcreekheritagefarm@ gmail.com, or at 870-428-5000.

By all common definitions, these chickens have become established as a breed. Instead of having to order new hybrid chicks every year—remember, hybrids are birds with parents of two different breeds, and if they reproduce there's no telling what you'll get—homesteaders can raise their own.

Can You Make Money?

Can you make money raising chickens, by building chicken coops, or in some other facet of the "new" chicken industry? There are obviously opportunities galore, open to forward-thinking people who can see the writing on the wall. The old ways of producing poultry products are endangered, if not doomed. No one can see into the future, but the people and operations described in this chapter give us a pretty revealing glimpse of it.

The Least You Need to Know

- Poultry production is facing great changes, which provide many new opportunities.
- Huge industrial-type agribusinesses are losing their monopolistic grip, as more consumers demand more organic-type products.
- One model for humane poultry production is the *Label Rouge* system in France.
- The McCraw family and their Ozark-farmed Black Walnut chickens provide a possible glimpse into a sustainable small-family chicken farm.

Chapter 3

Culling and Butchering

In This Chapter

◆ Reasons for killing a chicken

◆ Ways to carry out the task

◆ From chicken to meat

◆ Properly chilling the meat

In Chapter 1, I said there were four main reasons for raising chickens. Now, in lucky Chapter 13, I'll tell you the four reasons for killing a chicken and how to go about it with the least stress to you or the bird.

Death, a Fact of Life

Everything that lives, dies. Just as there are different reasons for raising a chicken, there are different reasons for killing it.

If you raise a bird for meat, the end is obvious. You will kill it, pluck it, eviscerate (gut) it, and probably either roast it whole or cut it into pieces for frying or broiling. You will do all this with respect, honoring the bird, because its flesh will become your flesh.

If you raised a bird to lay eggs, you'll have to make some decisions about how that career will end. A laying-type hen will be productive for a year or two. Most will then slack off. How much production drops, how much you're willing to pay for eggs at a reduced rate of lay, or maybe how loathe you are to butcher a hen that lays very few eggs all enter into the decision of whether to cull her and when. The meat of a bird at this stage will be suitable only for soup or stew, but that use likewise will honor the bird more than composting or deep burial.

If you breed and raise poultry to show, culls are part of the deal. Not every bird is show quality, even fewer are good enough to breed, and there will inevitably be a surplus. This requires culling, not for production as with layers, but for quality according to the *Standard of Perfection* for the breed. Such birds might or might not end up as meat.

And if you raise chickens as pets, the end will no doubt be even harder. Some diseases and conditions are mercifully swift, and you might be spared the task of euthanizing a creature you have grown attached to. But don't count on it. You don't want to see the bird suffer, and mercy-killing might be the only humane option. (Of course, you won't consider eating a bird that is sickly, whether it's a pet or not.)

In some places you can make an appointment to drop off a crate of live birds, then come back in a few days and pick up a box of neatly packaged frozen chicken. This probably won't work for one or two birds, and it's almost certainly not going to be economical. But it might be an easy way out. The other option is to do it yourself.

Getting Started

If the bird is going to become meat, the first step is to take it (or them) off feed. (If you are merely putting a bird out of its misery, skip to the section on killing, "The Hardest Part.") Put it in a pen with water but no feed, so the digestive tract will be empty when you reach that point. This step is not essential, but it makes the job easier.

Prepare your work area. You will want a clean and sturdy worktable, away from other poultry. You will need a pot of hot water, about 130°F, large enough to submerge the entire bird. Some people suggest having a container lined with a plastic bag for the *offal*, but then what will you do with the plastic? I prefer working on newspapers, then wrapping the waste in the paper. Paper can be composted; plastic can't.

You will want a sharp boning knife at a minimum, for when you eviscerate. As you gain experience, or if you're processing a number of birds, you might want to add a larger knife, poultry shears, or both for cutting up the carcass and maybe a pinfeather tool (which is also sold as a strawberry huller, although for most people a small knife and a thumb work just as well to pull out the tiny, pesky pinfeathers). Have a small, clean container for the *giblets*. A source of fresh running water is always handy when butchering.

def•i•ni•tion

The **offal** comprises the inedible guts of a chicken: crop, windpipe, etc. **Giblets** are edible internal organs, namely the heart, liver, and gizzard; commercial butchers often include the neck.

If you raised the birds specifically for meat, you have probably been watching the calendar and the feed supply as well as the birds, to determine when to butcher. A meat-type broiler should weigh close to 4½ or 5 pounds, at anywhere from 6 to 16 weeks of age, depending on breed and management, as we saw in the last chapter. It's not economical to feed a bird longer than necessary. If you have a few days' worth of feed left, you might wait until it's gone; if the choice is butchering a few days early or buying another sack of feed, you'll probably butcher early.

Cacklings

The usual advice is to avoid adding meat products to compost bins, primarily because of the attraction to dogs and other carnivores. Most landfills don't allow offal or dead animals, so you're between a rock and a hard place. Burying the guts as deeply as possible in an established compost pile or bin will usually do the trick. If that's not an option, you'll have to resort to burial, as deep as reasonably possible (about 3 feet) to deter diggers.

The Hardest Part

For most people, killing the bird is the worst part. Later on in the process there will be bloody hands, unpleasant things to touch, and even more unpleasant odors, but those are nothing compared to the discomfort of ending a life.

There are three common ways to dispatch a fowl. I have always used the traditional ax, or hatchet, and a chopping block. Many years ago *Countryside* magazine's cooking columnist told me there was a better way: dislocate the neck. You hold the bird by the legs with one hand and grasp the head with the other, cupping your hand under the beak. Then tilt the head back, and pull. The head will snap away from the neck, the bird will struggle, and it will be over.

Being short, she held the chicken by the legs with its head on the ground and placed a broomstick across the neck, then pulled, with the same result. For some reason, that procedure grossed me out more than holding the chicken by the legs, stretching the neck out on a block of wood, and chopping off the head. Different strokes for different folks.

Be advised that the ax method requires holding on to a flapping, struggling bird, spurting blood from a headless neck. Some people put it under a box or bushel basket until the flapping stops. Just letting it flop around makes a bloody mess of the feathers, and the wide area it flops in. Experts also tell me my method inhibits bleeding, which is considered important for good meat, and since the windpipe is severed, blood can get into the lungs. (I have never seen what I would call a lack of blood using this method.)

Maybe I've been doing it for too long, and I'm too old to change. If you're just starting out, you might be better off trying the dislocation method. You will still have to bleed the bird, but at least you can wait until it stops thrashing around. Hang it by its feet with a cord, cut the neck on both sides, and wait until the bleeding stops.

A third method falls somewhere between the other two and works especially well with large numbers of birds, say 20 or more, and a crew of helpers. It requires some preparation in the way of making "killing cones," unless you want to buy one or more for around $35 each.

When we ran a print shop, I made cones out of offset printing plates, but 16-inch-wide aluminum roof flashing 34 inches long will work. Measure 8½ inches in from both ends on one long edge. Cut from those marks to the corners on the opposite long side. Bringing the cut edges together will form your cone. Overlap those edges by about an inch, drill three holes through both edges along the seam, and rivet them together. Using these measurements (which can be varied for different size birds) the cone will have a top opening of about 9 inches, and a bottom of roughly 4 inches.

Fasten the cone to a tree or post (or the side of an outbuilding where a little blood won't matter). Place the bird into the cone head-first, grasp the head to stretch out the neck, and cut the jugular with a good, sharp knife. This method does not, or should not, cut the windpipe.

A professional would leave the head on until the bird is plucked (or picked or defeathered, and when your kids ask why a chicken is considered "dressed" after it's naked, you'll have to give the same answer I always did: I don't know). When I butcher any animal, I consider it still an animal as long as the head is on. Only with the head removed does it become "meat," and therefore easier to work with. Maybe that's another reason I use the hatchet. Take your choice.

Scalding

The next step is "scalding" the bird, which helps loosen the feathers. You'll need a kettle large enough to accommodate the whole bird: a large canning kettle or stock pot will do. Our biggest problem is heating the water. With a few birds, it's easiest to heat it on the kitchen stove and then carry it outside. When butchering more than three or four, the water will cool too much. You can refresh the scalding kettle with more hot water, but it's much handier to be able to reheat it at the work site. A propane unit such as a turkey fryer would be ideal, if you have one.

But watch the temperature. I don't mean with a thermometer, necessarily, because experts are going to tell you it should be anywhere from exactly 125°F to precisely 155°F, and if you're 2 degrees off their recommendation you'll ruin everything. If I heat the water to 155°F in the kitchen and take it outside, it has already cooled down before I dunk the first bird. It will get cooler by the time the second, third, and fourth get their turns. By then it might be 125°F. But by golly, at least one of those came pretty close to the right temperature! I can tell by how easily the feathers come out. And that's what counts. Within limits, it doesn't seem to make much difference.

Water that's too hot will blister the bird, and the skin will tear. Too cold, and the feathers won't want to come out. So we start out a bit on the hot side, and when the plucker can notice the job is becoming more difficult, even after redunking the bird, we add more hot water, or reheat it. This is all further complicated by the age of the bird, genetics, and the stage of its feathering, as well as the air temperature. In other words, it's largely a trial-and-error process. If you start to do this on a regular basis and use a thermostatically controlled dunk tank, you might arrive at your own preferred "perfect" temperature. For a couple of chickens, it's no big deal. Like thousands of us who have gone before, you'll get the job done even without the perfect temperature.

Cacklings

Adding a few drops of dishwashing soap to the scalding water helps the hot water penetrate dense, oily feathers.

Plucking

Holding the chicken by the feet, dunk it into the hot water with an up-and-down plunging action for maybe 20 to 30 seconds. Then try to pull out a few of the large wing feathers. If they don't release fairly easily, dunk the bird some more, until they do. (If that doesn't happen, the water is probably too cold.)

Wing feathers are usually the most difficult to pluck, so most people start with those, while the bird is still hot. Next comes the tail, followed by the breast and legs. If conditions are just right—the age of the bird, water temperature, and so on—the breast and leg feathers come out easily with a kind of slapping motion: you don't so much pluck or pull them as rub them off. That doesn't always work, but when it does, it's a thrill, especially if you have plucked countless chickens by laboriously pulling out the feathers.

> **Fox Alert**
>
> Notice that we're doing this outside. According to one lady I know who tried it, you do not want to pluck a chicken in your kitchen.

After all the actual feathers are gone, there are still pinfeathers—a whiskery stubble that can be excruciatingly difficult to remove. Some birds have more than others, depending on the stage of growth. Dark ones are more noticeable than white ones, which is why commercial meat birds are white. Today, many people who worry about cholesterol don't eat the skin anyway, so they don't worry about pinfeathers.

By now the chicken is starting to look like, well, a *chicken*, the supermarket kind. At least the store-bought kind from before World War II. It was called "New York dressed" and was plucked. That's it. The head and feet were still attached, and the housewife had to remove the entrails. Today, her granddaughter doesn't even know how to cut up a whole chicken!

> **Cocktail Conversation**
>
> Naturally there are mechanical pluckers and plans for making your own. I used a borrowed one once and wasn't impressed. Some models obviously work, for some people, but they hardly seem worthwhile for a few chickens. If you don't use a machine, you can console yourself by knowing that studies have indicated that machine plucking makes the meat tougher.

Incidentally, this is how chicken is "aged," which might be one of the reasons so many old-timers say chicken just doesn't taste like it used to. New York–dressed chicken can still be found in some Asian markets. You, too, can age a bird in this condition if you have space in a refrigerator or cooler. (The old practice of hanging it in a butcher shop window, sometimes even in the sun, is not recommended.)

A Footnote on Feet

At any rate, when you reach this point, the carcass doesn't look anything like the bird you knew, which makes it easier to gut it. If the head is still attached, cut it off now, with a stout knife, poultry shears, or garden secateurs. Leave the neck as long as possible: there isn't much meat on it, but it's a key ingredient in the stock pot. Cut off the feet at the joint between the scaly shank and the meaty drumstick. Bend it back and forth to get an idea of where the joint is—you're not cutting *through* bone, but *between* two of them. It's best to start from the front, trying to leave a flap of skin at the back, which prevents the meat from shrinking during cooking.

Save the feet. In the good old days, they were a special after-school treat. Special, because when food was scarce, they were much more valuable used in chicken stock, making them go further. Today they are a common staple in Asian cuisine, although some say it's an acquired taste. If you are a frugal person who likes Asian food and has acquired a taste for chicken feet, go for it.

Some people skin the feet at the same time as plucking the feathers, using the same scald. Others prefer to leave them until later and then put them in boiling water for a minute or so and pinch off the scales and toenail cuticles. Yet another method can be found on blogs and websites on oriental cooking, such as www.simplecookingideas. com, where Mary Ly suggests cutting off the claws, trimming off the hardened pads under the foot, then cleaning them thoroughly by rubbing with salt. Then she rinses them and boils them in water for five minutes.

A kosher recipe says to put the feet in a bowl, cover with boiling water, and let sit for at least 15 minutes. Then plunge them into ice water, and they'll be easy to peel with a sharp knife.

No matter how you clean them, chicken feet are one of the secret ingredients in the soup known as "Jewish Penicillin."

Cacklings

Some people relish the tail (pygostyle, pope's nose, parson's nose) as a treat. Others discard it. If you save it, remove the oil gland, located on the top, by making a cut about an inch above and down to the bone in a scooping motion, back to the tip of the tail.

Evisceration

With a small but sharp knife and the bird on its back, make an incision from the keel bone (breast bone) down to the vent. Try holding the skin taut with one hand and cutting the skin stretched between your thumb and index finger. Cut just into the skin, not into the intestines underneath. When you come to the vent, reach into the incision with one finger to hold the intestine out of the way, and cut around the vent.

Next, reach into the opening and feel your way around the cavity walls to loosen the membranes that hold the intestines. When you can get a decent handhold on the gizzard (which is harder than the other parts), grasp it and start pulling in a slow, steady motion. Everything, or almost everything, will come out at once. Examine the mass for the liver and heart. (Both are like the feet, in that most uppity modern people will have nothing to do with them. But then, those people don't butcher their own chickens, either.) Cut off the liver but be very careful of the attached gall bladder. Remove this, carefully, by cutting a part of the liver off with it, to avoid breaking the sac and contaminating the liver with the green bile. If that happens despite your care, immediately wash the liver in plenty of cold water. (Some people don't bother washing it: they just toss it, saying it will taste bitter. Maybe they don't use enough butter and garlic when frying chicken livers.)

> **Fox Alert**
>
> Don't use livers in soup stock: it will make the soup bitter, even if the gall bladder wasn't broken. But lightly fried or roasted, they're delicious.

Cut the gizzard loose and then slice it in half. Take an interesting and instructive moment to examine the contents. Peel off the tough, grit-laden lining.

To remove the crop and windpipe, slit the skin along the back of the neck, peel it down the front of the bird to the crop, and cut below the crop. Pull it out. Wash the carcass thoroughly in cold running water.

Chilling

The meat must be chilled quickly, especially in warm or hot weather. How chilling is accomplished has recently taken on increased importance. One reason is that more consumers have been made aware of the method used by the leading commercial processors. The fresh meat is dumped into vats of water laden with the debris from intestines ruptured by mechanical evisceration, including fecal material, and it soaks in that sewage. The water contains salmonella and campylobacter bacteria. Some writers describe vats with several inches of sludge on the bottom.

If this doesn't ruin your appetite, then also be aware that federal regulations allow chickens to absorb up to 12 percent of their body weight in water from the contaminated immersion bath. That means that 12 percent of what you pay for a chicken is for contaminated water. That's also why the chicken police want you to thoroughly wash everything raw chicken comes in contact with and to cook it thoroughly. Some chicken is reportedly washed in chlorine, and now it's okay to irradiate it, too. Maybe it would be better to just butcher your own so you know it's done right.

The University of Nebraska Food Science and Technology Department found a "significant reduction" in salmonella and campylobacter in air-cooled chickens, compared to water-cooled. Recall that in Chapter 12 "air cooling" was mentioned as a requirement for *Label Rouge* chickens. The problems associated with water cooling on a large scale are one reason to prefer air cooling over water cooling, but there is also a flavor factor. Adding 12 percent water does not enhance flavor—especially when the water is contaminated.

So, cool your freshly butchered chicken. But wash it thoroughly in running water before placing it in a container with others, and keep the water running, slowly, in the container, both to lower the temperature and to keep it clean. And as soon as the meat is cooled, remove it from the water and refrigerate it.

Tough Meat

Backyard chicken raisers who butcher their own chickens are frequently dismayed by how tough the meat is. There are several explanations for tough meat, but toughness can often be traced to sending the freshly killed bird directly to the freezer. Meat becomes tough soon after butchering, and must "age" before it relaxes and becomes tender. Some old-timers corresponding with *Countryside* magazine have sworn that the best chicken is New York–dressed and hung, unrefrigerated, for several days. You can imagine what we heard from health professionals. But storing a fresh chicken in the refrigerator for a few days is not only okay, but recommended. Figure one to three days before freezing the meat, or up to five if you're using it fresh.

Cocktail Conversation

All this would obviously be much clearer and easier if you could have an experienced mentor on hand (who might or might not agree with all of my methods). If you don't know any chicken butchers, maybe a hunter would be willing to help. Lacking that, you'll find a good website at www.themodernhomestead.us/article/Butchering-Ready. html#pagetop, where poultry guru Harvey Ussery explains his technique, with photos.

The Least You Need to Know

♦ There are several reasons to kill chickens: for meat, because of reduced egg-laying production, because of lack of show quality, or because of illness.

♦ Three common ways to dispatch a fowl include the ax-and-chopping-block method; dislocating the neck; and with a knife, using "killing cones."

♦ Feathers are easier to pluck if the chicken is dunked in scalding water, about 130°F.

♦ Store-bought chicken is not as safe and sanitary as the industry would like you to think it is: you can do better at home.

♦ Putting freshly butchered chickens directly into the freezer results in tough meat. Chill them for several days first.

14

Eggs in the Kitchen

In This Chapter

◆ Eggs aren't just for breakfast

◆ Nutritional value

◆ Preserving eggs

◆ The egg in lore and legend

You don't need a book on raising chickens to tell you how to cook an egg. The original *Boston Cooking School* cookbook, written by Fannie Farmer in 1896, had nearly 50 different recipes for eggs; the latest *Joy of Cooking* has almost as many; and the famed *Escoffier* cookbook has more than either of those. And that's not counting recipes in which eggs play a minor role, such as in cakes and pastries.

But here are a few egg facts you probably won't find in your cookbooks.

Eggs: Everywhere

You undoubtedly eat more eggs than you realize. They're a multifunctional ingredient used in many food products, some of which might surprise you.

At home you might use them to glaze bakery, emulsify salad dressings, and bind ingredients in such dishes as meat loaf. Eggs are used to thicken, clarify, and leaven other foods, and they retard crystallization in confections and frosting. In food manufacturing, egg "foaming" is crucial in angel cakes and other baked goods. The volume of vigorously beaten albumen, or egg white, expands or foams six to eight times. Egg foams are essential for soufflés, meringues, and many other goods.

Cocktail Conversation

Egg white isn't white (until it's cooked), but opalescent, or somewhat cloudy. That's caused by carbon dioxide. The carbon dioxide escapes as the egg ages, so the albumen of older eggs is more transparent than that of fresher eggs. In another sign of age (along with air cell size and the chalazae), egg white tends to thin out as the protein content changes. It becomes "runny."

Egg gelatin is utilized in meat products, custards, and surimi (minced fish used to manufacture imitation seafood such as lobster or crab). Yolk and whole-egg products provide emulsification in mayonnaise and sauces.

The biggest egg users are the baking industry, makers of sauces and dressings, pasta manufacturers, and producers of dry mixes. These eggs are frozen, liquid, refrigerated, or dried. You'll never see a Grade B egg in the marketplace, because they all go into these manufactured goods.

One basis for determining grade is the size of the air cell. In a freshly layed, still-warm egg, the shell is completely filled. As it cools, the contents contract, the inner shell membrane separates from the outer shell, and the air cell forms. In a Grade AA egg this cell can't exceed $\frac{1}{8}$ inch in depth, or about the size of a dime. Grade A eggs have larger air cells, up to $\frac{3}{16}$ inch deep and about the size of a quarter. There is no air cell size limit on Grade B eggs.

Air enters the egg (and carbon dioxide escapes) through anywhere from 7,000 to 17,000 microscopic pores in the shell. The "bloom" of an unwashed egg, the coating applied to the egg just before it's layed, blocks these pores, which is why unwashed eggs stay fresher longer.

Cocktail Conversation

USDA inspected eggs are required to have the Julian date of packing displayed on the carton. (In Julian dating, Jan. 1 is 1 and Dec. 31 is 365.) Expiration dates are not required, but if they're used, they can't be more than 30 days beyond the packing date.

Eggs with blood spots and abnormal shells are also kept out of retail markets, but being edible, are used in manufacturing.

How recently the egg was layed is only one factor in determining quality. The American Egg Board advises that a week-old egg, held under ideal conditions, can be "fresher" than a day-old egg left at room temperature.

> **Fox Alert**
>
> Eggs must be refrigerated for safety and to preserve freshness. Ideal conditions are temperatures below 40°F and a relative humidity of 70 to 80 percent.

The Nutritious Egg

You're aware that eggs are extremely nutritious, and you probably know they contain the proteins against which other foods are measured. That's because eggs contain all the amino acids (which proteins are made of) required by the human body. By weight, eggs are 12.5 percent protein, with more than half in the albumen.

Vitamins and Minerals

Eggs contain most of the recognized vitamins except vitamin C. They're a good source of all the B vitamins. The yolk contains a higher proportion of the egg's vitamins than the white, with the exception of riboflavin and niacin. All of the egg's vitamins A, D, and E are in the yolk. (Eggs are one of the few foods naturally containing vitamin D.)

They also contain most of the minerals needed for human health, especially iodine and phosphorus, but also zinc, selenium, and iron.

What About Cholesterol?

All the to-do about eggs and cholesterol is largely in the past. More recent studies show that dietary cholesterol doesn't necessarily relate to blood cholesterol. Since most of the cholesterol in your body is manufactured in your body, some medical authorities now say you'd have to eat five jumbo eggs a day to notice much difference in your cholesterol level. Unfortunately, after 30 years of hearing that eggs increase serum cholesterol levels, it will take a while to convince some people otherwise. Unfortunate, because in addition to high-quality protein and a variety of vitamins and minerals, eggs are rich in dietary lutein, which might prevent age-related macular disease, and they provide choline, which has been connected with fetal development.

Claims that some eggs have less cholesterol than others either don't stand up to rigorous scientific testing, or the difference is insignificant. Likewise, science has found no basis for choosing organic eggs, or fertile eggs. Like the shell color—which has no bearing on the taste or quality of what's inside—these are strictly personal preferences based on other criteria.

Size Makes a Difference

Size is something else. It doesn't matter much if you're making an omelet, but it can make a difference in some recipes, and for people who buy eggs, there is often a difference in the price per pound. The United States Department of Agriculture recognizes these egg sizes:

Size	Mass per Egg	Weight per Dozen
Jumbo	More than 2.5 oz.	30 oz.
X-Large	More than 2.25 oz.	27 oz.
Large	More than 2 oz.	24 oz.
Medium	More than 1.75 oz.	21 oz.
Small	More than 1.5 oz.	18 oz.
Peewee	More than 1.25 oz.	15 oz.

Cocktail Conversation

Egg consumption in the United States peaked in 1945, at 402 per person. It bottomed out in 1995 to 175 due to cholesterol concerns, climbed back up to 258.1 (as of 2006) with the popularity of low-carbohydrate diets, and fell back to an estimated 250 for 2009. That's roughly 6.5 billion eggs a year, just in the United States.

Note that these sizes have nothing to do with USDA grades (AA, A, and B), which are based on quality and appearance.

If small eggs cost more than 60 percent of the price of jumbos, the jumbos are a better deal. Most recipes call for large eggs, so if you're making a cake with pullet or bantam peewee eggs, or with jumbos, it's helpful to know that three large eggs are equal to just about five peewees, that it will take seven small eggs to replace five large ones, and that three large eggs can be replaced by two jumbos.

Hard-Boiled Eggs ... Aren't

Or they shouldn't be. Boiling an egg makes it tough and rubbery. (Eggs should be cooked gently, by any method.) Hard-*cooked* is a much better term.

The widely accepted way to hard-cook eggs is to place them in a saucepan in a single layer, add enough water to barely cover them, and slowly bring the water to a boil. Some people add salt to the water. When it starts to boil, cover the pan, remove it from the heat, and let it sit for 15 to 20 minutes, depending on the size. Then remove the eggs with a slotted spoon and immediately plunge them into very cold, even ice water. Bring the water in the pan to a boil again, then dip the chilled eggs, one at a time, in the boiling water for exactly 10 seconds. This will cause the shell to expand, separating it from the white. Crack the shell all over by rolling it on a hard surface and peel it at once. If you start at the big end, which you now know is where the air cell is located, peeling it will be easier.

"Boiled" or "cooked," these eggs are often a source of frustration for new chicken farmers, because fresh eggs are almost impossible to peel.

As we have seen, a fresh egg fills nearly the entire shell, with little or no air space. When such an egg is cooked, it sticks to the shell. Try to peel it, and you'll peel off layers of the white as well, leading to the frustration.

So, ironic as it might seem, after bragging so loudly about the fine quality of our fresh home-grown eggs, we must sheepishly admit that for hard-cooked eggs, a little aging is a good thing. About a week should do it. Wait too long, and the yolk will be off-center, as the white and chalazae deteriorate. This causes other problems, such as a very thin and weak layer of white on one side. Leaving fresher eggs at room temperature overnight will help.

The Freshness Test

Today nobody worries much about how to tell whether an egg is fresh, but when most people had their own chickens and it was common to find a nest hidden in the haymow or under a bush, that information was important, and most cookbooks included it.

An egg's freshness can be augured from the degree to which it sinks or floats. A freshly layed egg, which has no air cell, sinks to the bottom of a container of water. When the egg is about a week old, the blunt end (where the air cell is located) will rise slightly off the bottom of the container. As the egg ages the angle increases until, by about two or three weeks, it will stand almost vertical in the water, blunt end up. A really old egg will float.

Preserving Eggs

When you produce your own eggs, you'll sometimes have more than you can use, and sometimes you'll run out. Chickens lay fewer eggs in the winter; they stop laying when they molt; and there are other vagaries. This problem was even worse for our ancestors, before there were electric lights and improved breeds of layers, to say nothing of mechanical refrigeration. They prepared for the egg droughts by preserving them during the floods. You can have fun doing the same, even if you don't have to.

Salted Eggs

There are uses for hard-cooked eggs in addition to the usual deviled eggs and garnishes. *Soleier*, a German favorite (it goes well with peasant bread and beer), is sometimes simply referred to as salted eggs. Crackle the shells of six hard-cooked eggs but don't peel them. Put them into a wide-mouth 1-quart canning jar and cover them with 3 cups of water previously boiled with ¼ cup salt (add some onion skins if you want them more colorful) and cooled. Refrigerate for at least 24 hours.

Pickled Eggs

Eggs can be pickled in sweet, sour, or spicy brines. If stored in the brine and refrigerated, they will keep for several months, so this is another good use for those abundant spring eggs.

First cover the eggs with cold water, bring to a boil, cover and turn off the heat, and let them sit for 15 to 20 minutes depending on size. Cool the eggs in ice or cold running water, and peel them. Put them in a jar that can be closed tightly and pour the hot pickling solution (recipes follow) over them. Seal the jar and refrigerate. It will take a week to cure small eggs, from two to four weeks for medium and large.

These recipes should provide enough pickling solution for a dozen eggs. To prepare, heat the mixture to near boiling and simmer for 5 to 10 minutes.

Beet Red Eggs

1 cup red beet juice

1½ cups cider vinegar

1 teaspoon brown sugar

A few small, sliced, canned beets may be added

Dilled Eggs

1½ cups white vinegar

1 cup water

¾ teaspoon dill seed

¼ teaspoon white pepper

3 teaspoons salt

¼ teaspoon mustard seed

½ teaspoon onion juice

½ teaspoon garlic, minced

Spicy Eggs

1½ cups apple cider

1 cup white vinegar

2 teaspoons salt

1 teaspoon mixed pickling spice

1 clove garlic, peeled

½ onion, sliced

½ teaspoon mustard seed

Freezing Eggs

Eggs can be frozen, but the yolks will coagulate unless you stir in 1 teaspoon of salt, or 1 tablespoon of sugar or corn syrup, with each cup of yolks. (The choice of salt or sugar depends on what the eggs will be used for; for example, sugar for baked goods calling for sugar. Be sure to label them!) The whites can be frozen as is.

Whites and yolks can be frozen together by mixing one dozen eggs with one teaspoon of salt or one tablespoon of sugar. This mixture can be frozen in a six-muffin tin, then removed and stored in plastic freezer bags. Each "muffin" is two eggs. Thaw completely before using.

Drying Eggs

Dry only perfect, very fresh eggs. They must be separated, or they'll turn green. Add 1 teaspoon of cream of tartar to 12 whites, beat to a stiff meringue, and place it on a sheet of Teflon or plastic wrap on the dryer tray. When crisp, grind to a powder with a rolling pin and store in moisture-proof bags.

Beat the yolks until thick and foamy and pour the batter on a tray in a very thin layer. You might want to stir up the crust that will form for more even drying. Eggs should dry in about 12 to 18 hours at 115°F.

Cacklings

The main secret to preserving eggs is starting out with unwashed eggs (the bloom has not been removed) with absolutely no hairline cracks or chips.

Some older books mention preserving eggs in waterglass, or sodium silicate, available through a druggist. In the days before refrigeration, a solution of nine parts water to one of waterglass preserved eggs for up to a year. However, eggs stored in airtight containers at between 35°F and 40°F will keep just as well, or better.

Truly Amazing

The egg is amazing, and valuable, because of its many culinary uses and nutritional value, but its role in human history and culture goes far beyond that. The egg is strongly associated with creation myths in many cultures, and many storied gods and goddesses—as well as a few demons—were believed to have sprung from eggs. The egg represents rebirth in many religious traditions, and it was a key element in alchemy. Historically, the egg had many medical uses, and today influenza and yellow fever vaccines are propagated in eggs. Eggs are decorated by children; by painters, carvers, and other artists; and by famous goldsmiths such as Carl Faberge. Countless fables, songs, stories, traditions, and customs surround the plain, simple egg.

And the egg is only a small part of what the chicken has given us. This under-appreciated bird feeds not only our bodies but our very humanness. From the very first domesticated fighting cocks, to the birds contributing to cancer research and new microchips today, to who-knows-what tomorrow, chickens have been a part of our civilization. We wouldn't be who or what we are without them.

Have you hugged your chicken today?

The end.

(Photo: Melissa A. Knight, Ashland City, Tennessee)

The Least You Need to Know

- ◆ Eggs are important in many manufactured foods; you might not even realize you're eating them.

- ◆ Eggs are nature's most perfect food and contain the protein other foods are measured against.

- ◆ Under optimum storage conditions, an egg should be edible for a month after being layed, and some will keep as long as a year.

- ◆ Eggs play a large role in most human cultures.

Glossary

ABA   American Bantam Association.

alektorophobia   Fear of chickens.

AMBC   American Minor Breeds Conservancy. An organization devoted to saving endangered breeds of domestic livestock, including chickens.

American Standard of Perfection   The handbook of the American Poultry Association describing and picturing the ideal characteristics against which each recognized breed is judged.

APA   American Poultry Association.

avian   Pertaining to birds (Class *Aves*).

bantam   A smaller version of a large chicken, ¼ to ⅕ the size; a small chicken with no large counterpart.

barnyard chicken   A chicken of mixed or uncertain parentage.

bedding   Litter; any material used to absorb liquids in manure (straw, wood shavings, shredded paper, ground corncobs, etc.).

biddy   Old hen (slang).

biosecurity   Measures taken to prevent disease.

bloom   The final protective coating on an eggshell, which is removed when eggs are washed.

breed   (Noun) An established group with similar characteristics that, when mated together, produce offspring with the same characteristics. (Verb) To mate, for reproduction.

breeder   A person who breeds chickens; a chicken used for reproduction rather than meat or eggs for food.

broiler   A young chicken weighing about 4½ pounds; fryer.

brood   (Verb) Provide care for chicks. (Noun) A batch of chicks.

brooder   A box or other enclosure where chicks are protected and cared for.

broody   Used to describe a hen that wants to sit on eggs.

buff   A medium shade of orange-yellow with a rich golden cast.

candle   To examine the contents of an intact egg with the use of a light.

cannibalism   The act of chickens pecking at and eating each other or eggs.

capon   A castrated rooster, creating a large and tender roasting fowl.

carrier   An individual that shows no symptoms of a disease but can transmit the disease to others.

clean-legged   Having featherless shanks (lower part of the leg).

cloaca   The terminal region of the gut, into which empty the intestinal, urinary, and genital canals.

clutch   A setting or group of eggs for hatching.

coccidiosis   An intestinal disease caused by a parasitic sporozoan.

coccidiostat   A drug that prevents or treats coccidiosis; the specific drug and dosage vary with intent and the coccidia species involved.

cock   A male chicken; rooster.

cockerel   A male chicken under one year old.

comb   The fleshy red-to-purple (depending on breed) growth on top of a chicken's head, seen in various shapes and forms (also depending on breed), but larger in the rooster of any given breed.

compost   (Noun) A mixture of decayed organic matter used to enrich soil. (Verb) To mix organic materials together in such a way as to achieve controlled decomposition.

conformation   The general shape and structure of a body.

coop   Chicken house.

crop   A sac (an enlarged part of the gullet), located on a bird's chest, in which food is temporarily stored immediately after it's eaten.

crossbreed   (Verb) To mate two birds of different breeds. (Noun) The offspring of such a mating.

cull   (Verb) To eliminate an undesirable individual from the flock based on productivity, a standard of perfection, health, etc. (Noun) The bird itself.

debeak   To cut off a portion of the upper beak to prevent cannibalism.

diatomaceous earth (DE)   A light, porous sedimentary rock composed of the shells of diatoms, used to control insects and other pests.

down   Very fluffy short feathers.

droppings   Manure.

dust bath   Refers to the chicken's habit of rolling in dust or dry soil to control mites and lice and to remove excess oil from the feathers.

ear lobes   Fleshy patches of bare skin below the ears, varying in size and shape according to breed.

egg tooth   A horny growth on a chick's upper beak, used to break through the eggshell at hatching time.

embryo   A fertilized ovum; a chick before it's hatched.

encephalomalacia   Softening of the brain.

excreta   Waste matter eliminated; bird manure consisting of both feces and uric acid.

exhibition breeds   Chickens bred and kept for appearance rather than egg or meat production, usually to be displayed at competitive poultry shows.

feather-legged   Having feathers growing on the shanks (lower part of the leg).

fecal   Having to do with solid bodily waste.

feces   Solid bodily waste.

fertile   (Egg) One containing a live embryo. (Chicken) One capable of reproducing.

flock   Any number of chickens living together as a group.

forage   (Verb) To scavenge for food on free-range. (Noun) Food found by scavenging.

fowl   Any domestic bird; poultry.

free-range   Refers to chickens allowed to roam at will.

fryer   A tender young chicken weighing about 4½ pounds; broiler.

gizzard   A very strong muscular organ that, with the aid of grit, grinds up a bird's food for further digestion.

grit   Small stones or other hard materials a bird ingests to help grind food in the gizzard.

hackles   The feathers on the rear and sides of the neck; usually different in shape and structure according to sex.

hatch   (Verb) To emerge from an egg. (Noun) A group of chicks that emerge from their eggs at roughly the same time.

hen   A female chicken more than one year old.

hybrid   Any bird or animal with parents of two different breeds.

immunity   Resistance to a particular disease, often as the result of an inoculation.

incubate   To hatch fertile eggs.

incubation period   Time required for an egg to hatch; for chickens, normally 21 days.

incubator   A heated machine for hatching eggs.

keel   Breastbone.

litter   Bedding; straw, ground corncobs, wood shavings, or similar absorbent materials on the floor of a coop.

mate   To breed; to engage in sex.

Marek's Disease   A widespread, highly contagious virus disease of chickens, commonly controlled by vaccination upon hatching.

milo   Grain sorghum.

mite   A tiny bothersome parasite.

molt   (Verb) To lose old feathers and grow new ones. (Noun) The process or time during which feathers are shed.

nest   A place where a chicken lays eggs.

nest egg   An artificial egg, usually made of wood or plastic (but sometimes just a golf ball), used to encourage hens to lay eggs in a certain place.

nestbox   A box or similar enclosure provided as a secure place for a chicken to lay eggs.

oocysts   The eggs of certain parasites.

parasite   An organism that lives in or on another organism offering no benefit to the host.

pasting   The result of loose droppings that stick to the body and feathers in the vent area; also known as "pasty bottom."

pecking order   The social ranking in a flock of chickens.

pen   A fenced-in area.

perch   (Noun) An elevated place where chickens sit, especially to sleep. (Verb) To sit on a roost.

pinfeathers   Very short, quill-like, new feather growth.

pip   (Verb) To cut through an eggshell in the process of hatching. (Noun) The crack or hole created during hatching.

plumage   Feathers.

poultry   Any domestic fowl, including chickens, ducks, geese, turkeys, and guineas.

precocial   The ability of a chick to walk and feed itself within a few hours after hatching.

predator   A meat-eating bird or animal that kills other birds or animals, such as chickens.

producer   A company or individual that raises chickens for meat or eggs.

pullet   A female chicken less than one year old.

purebred   The offspring of two parents of the same breed.

ration   Total amount of feed containing all essential nutrients.

roaster   A meat chicken weighing 4 to 6 pounds.

roost   (Noun) The place, usually elevated and slender like a tree branch, where chickens sleep. (Verb) The act of sitting in such a place; also perch.

rooster   A male chicken more than one year old.

saddle   The chicken's back, between the wings and tail.

scales   Small, hard, overlapping fishlike plates covering a chicken's shanks and toes.

scratch   (Noun) Whole grains fed to chickens. (Verb) To scrape the ground with the feet in search of food.

setting hen   One who sits on eggs to hatch them.

sex link   A hybrid chicken whose sex can be determined at hatching by coloring rather than genital inspection.

sexed   Newly hatched chicks that are separated into pullets and cockerels.

shank   The lower part of the leg, below the drumstick.

spurs   Stiff, usually sharp and pointy growths on the rear inner side of a rooster's shanks, used for fighting.

standard (of perfection)   Description of the ideal specimen of a particular breed, as agreed upon by a committee of breeders.

started pullet   A young female chicken, past the brooding stage but not quite ready to start laying eggs.

starter   Feed or ration, usually in the form of crumbles, formulated for the nutritional needs of just-hatched chicks.

straight run   Unsexed chicks, just as they come from the incubator (and the hen).

strain   A closely bred or line-bred group of chickens showing great uniformity within their breed.

type   The general size and shape of a chicken.

uropygium   The bony and fleshy knob from which tail feathers grow.

variety   Subdivision within a breed, often indicating color, comb type, or other visible characteristic.

vent   The opening to the cloaca.

wattles   The two fleshy appendages like combs that grow under the chin.

Resources

Following is a sampling of resources on raising chickens to get you started.

Books

Aldrovandi, Ulisse. *Aldrovandi on Chickens*. 1600. University of Oklahoma Press, 1963. Translated and edited by L. R. Lind.
You aren't likely to actually read this hard-to-find book, but almost every chicken writer mentions it, so you should at least be aware that it's a fascinating and comprehensive examination of the chicken, from every angle, from ancient times until it was written in 1600.

American Standard of Perfection. American Poultry Association (updated periodically).
Pricey, but essential for knowing the recognized breeds, disqualifications, etc.

Bantam Standard (updated periodically).
A must-have for showing bantams.

Burnham, George P. *The History of the Hen Fever: A Humorous Record*. Reprinted by The University of Michigan Library, 1855.
Quaintly funny history.

Damerow, Gail. *The Chicken Health Handbook*. North Adams, MA: Storey Publishing, 1994.
Way more than most normal people want to know about chicken health, essential for the others, and handy for all.

———. *Storey's Guide to Raising Chickens*. North Adams, MA: Storey Publishing, 1995.
Very detailed how-to info.

———. *Your Chickens: A Kid's Guide to Raising and Showing*. North Adams, MA: Storey Publishing, 1993.
Just what the title says, but not only for kids.

Ekarius, Carol. *Storey's Illustrated Guide to Poultry Breeds*. North Adams, MA: Storey Publishing, 2007.
More than 128 gorgeous color photos of birds.

Foreman, Patricia. *City Chicks: Keeping Micro-Flocks of Laying Hens as Garden Helpers, Compost Makers, Bio-Recyclers and Local Food Suppliers*. Buena Vista, VA: Good Earth Publications, 2009.
Covers way more than chickens, as the title implies.

Heinrichs, Christine. *How to Raise Chickens—Everything You Need to Know*. Osceola, WI: Voyageur Press, 2007.
The basics, and much more.

———. *How to Raise Poultry*. Osceola, WI: Voyageur Press, 2009.
This one covers everything from pigeons to ostriches.

Kilarski, Barbara. *Keep Chickens: Tending Small Flocks in Cities, Suburbs, and Other Small Spaces*. North Adams, MA: Storey Publishing, 2003.
The basics, from a city chick, illustrated with interesting vintage poultry ads.

Lee, Andy, and Patricia Foreman. *Chicken Tractor: The Permaculture Guide to Happy Hens and Healthy Soil*. Buena Vista, VA: Good Earth Publications, 1994.
One of the classics, heavy on the healthy soil part.

Luttmann, Rick, and Gail Luttmann. *Chickens in Your Backyard: A Beginner's Guide*. Emmaus, PA: Rodale Press, 1976.
An oldie but goodie.

Padgham, Jody, ed. *Raising Poultry on Pasture*. Boyd, WI: The American Pastured Poultry Producers, 2006.
A series of articles on many topics from members of the APPP.

Pangman, Judy. *Chicken Coops: 45 Building Plans for Housing Your Flock*. North Adams, MA: Storey Publishing, 2006.
"Plans" is a misnomer, but it's a dandy idea-starter.

Percy, Pam. *The Field Guide to Chickens*. Osceola, WI: Voyageur Press, 2006.
Very interesting, profusely illustrated (mostly paintings) overview on chickens.

Rogers, David, and Toni-Marie Astin. *Long-Tailed Fowl: Their History and Care*. www.countrywhatnotgardens.com/book.html; 2007.
About Japanese chickens.

Rossier, Jay, and Geoff Hansen. *Living with Chickens*. Guilford, CT: The Lyons Press, 2002.
Beautiful photography.

Salatin, Joel. *Pastured Poultry Profit$*. Swoope, VA: Polyface, Inc., 1993.
A classic essential for even the smallest commercial producer.

Sheasley, Bob. *Home to Roost: A Backyard Farmer Chases Chickens Through the Ages*. New York: St. Martin's Press, 2008.
A newspaper editor meets Aldrovandi in a literary poultry potpourri.

Smith, Page, and Charles Daniel. *The Chicken Book*. Athens, GA: University of Georgia Press, 1975.
My personal favorite book on the *whole* chicken, as Aldrovandi treats it.

Hatcheries

Here's a random selection of both large and small suppliers of both general and specialized chickens, just to get you started.

Braggs Mountain Poultry
1558 Kreider Road
Ft. Gibson, OK 74454
www.braggsmountainpoultry.com
Braggs Mountain Buff: "The Golden Hen that lays the jumbo brown eggs."

Cackle Hatchery
PO Box 529
Lebanon, MO 65536
417-532-4581
www.cacklehatchery.com
More than 180 varieties of poultry.

Clearview Stock Farm & Hatchery
Box 399
Gratz, PA 17030
717-365-3234
Poultry of all types.

Hoffman Hatchery, Inc.
PO Box 129
Gratz, PA 17030
717-365-3694
www.hoffmanhatchery.com
Free catalog.

Ideal Poultry Breeding Farms, Inc.
PO Box 591
Cameron, TX 76520
254-697-6677
www.idealpoultry.com
Family-owned since 1937; basic and rare breeds.

J. M. Hatchery
178 Lowry Rd.
New Holland, PA 17557
717-354-5950 or 717-330-3247
Label Rouge–type broiler chicks.

Moyer's Chicks
266 E. Paletown Rd.
Quakertown, PA 19851
215-536-3155
www.moyerschicks.com
Broilers, layers, pullets.

Myers Poultry Farm
966 Ragers Hill Rd.
South Fork, PA 15956
814-539-7026
"Providing a product that 'meats' your needs." Free catalog.

MT-DI Poultry Farm
1209 South Catherine Rd.
Altoona, PA 16602
814-942-7024
E-mail: mtdifarm@atlanticbb.net
Label Rouge–type broiler chicks.

Mt. Healthy Hatcheries
1-800-451-5603
www.mthealthy.com
Since 1924; free color catalog.

Noll's Poultry Farm
Kleinfeltersville, PA
717-949-3560
Slower-growing broiler strains.

Ridgeway Hatchery
PO Box 306
LaRue, OH 43332
www.ridgewayhatchery.com
Since 1925; free catalog.

Whelp Hatchery
PO Box 77
Bancroft, IA 50517
www.whelphatchery.com
"Cornish Rock broilers are our specialty."

Whitmore Farm
10720 Dern Rd.
Emmitsburg, MD 21727
301-447-3611
www.whitmorefarm.com
E-mail: info@whitmorefarm.com
Delawares and other heritage breeds.

Chickens and Poultry Supplies

Hoover's Hatchery
1-800-247-7014
www.hoovershatchery.com
Broilers, layers, equipment, and medications, since 1944.

Meyer Hatchery
626 State Route 89
Polk, OH 44866
1-888-568-9755
www.meyerhatchery.com
115 varieties, minimum order 3;
supplies.

Murray McMurray Hatchery
www.mcmurrayhatchery.com/index.html
"The world's largest rare breed
hatchery."

My Pet Chicken
www.mypetchicken.com
Chickens, coops, supplies, books.

Randall Burkey Company
1-800-531-1097
www.randallburkey.com
Sells everything you could want or need for poultry, including chicks, eggs, and coops.

Stromberg's Chicks and Gamebirds Unlimited
PO Box 400
Pine River, MN 56474
218-587-2222
www.strombergschickens.com
Chickens and other birds, equipment and supplies, books and videos.

Poultry Housing and Supplies

Critter-Cages.com
305 N. Harbor Blvd.
San Pedro, CA 90731
310-832-9981
E-mail: order@critter-cages.com
Coops, wire mesh, incubators.

Fleming Outdoors
5480 Hwy. 94
Ramer, AL 36069
1-800-624-4493
www.flemingoutdoors.com
Equipment, including transportation coops.

Foy's Pet Supplies
3185 Bennett's Run Road
Beaver Falls, PA 15010
877-355-7727
www.foyspigeonsupplies.com
Chicken coops, nests, drinkers, feeders.

HenSpa
3900 Milton Hwy.
Ringgold, VA 24586
1-800-783-6344
http://henspa.com
Coops.

Horizon Structures
5075 Lower Valley Rd.
Atglen, PA 19310
1-888-44SHEDS
www.horizonstructures.com/mini_coop.asp
Finished coops and kits.

Kencove Farm Fence Supplies
113 W. 5th St.
Earl Park, IN 47942
1-800-536-2683
www.kencove.com
Electric netting and chargers.

Little Cottage Co.
4070 State Road 39
Berlin, OH 44610
330-893-4212
www.cottagekits.com
Chicken coops.

Octashed
4282 Winklepleck Road NW
Sugarcreek, OH 44681
330-852-0519
www.octashed.com
The Octa-Coop.

Omlet
1-866-653-8872
www.omlet.us
Eglu chicken coop includes hens, feed, and advice.

Poultryman's Supply
PO Box 612
Columbus, IN 47202
812-603-7722
www.poultrymansupply.com
Equipment, medications, books, brooders, etc.

Premier 1 Supplies
2031 300th Street
Washington, IA 52353
1-800-282-6631
www.premier1supplies.com
Fencing and poultry equipment.

Chicken Websites

http://home.centurytel.net/thecitychicken/chickenlaws.html, or a more technical site, http://www.municode.com/   Updated laws concerning chickens, by city.

www.themodernhomestead.us/   Practical, commonsense info on raising chickens for home use or small-scale commercial production; referred to in the text for butchering, and raising worms and fly maggots for chicken feed.

madcitychickens.com/index.html   Madison, Wisconsin's "poultry underground."

www.poultryhelp.com/link-eggs.html   General info with many links.

www.eggbid.com/   Online poultry auction.

www.feathersite.com/Poultry/BRKPoultryPage.html   One of the best all-around poultry sites.

www.ansi.okstate.edu/poultry/chickens/   Devoted to pictures and descriptions of specific breeds.

www.ithaca.edu/staff/jhenderson/chooks/chlinks.html   Excellent site, with links to everything chickenish imaginable.

www.ianrpubs.unl.edu/epublic/live/ec282/build/ec282.pdf   4-H and showing.

www.backyardchickens.com/   Good general info, forum.

http://insected.arizona.edu/flyrear.htm   How to make a fly trap.

http://agr.wa.gov/FoodAnimal/animalhealth/StateVets.aspx   List of all state veterinarians.

Publications

Backyard Poultry
145 Industrial Dr.
Medford, WI 54451
www.backyardpoultrymag.com

Fancy Fowl USA
159 Creekside Drive
Anderson, AL 35610

Feather Fancier (Canada)
www.featherfancier.on.ca

Poultry Press
www.poultrypress.com

Clubs and Associations

Just a random sampling:

American Bantam Association
Box 127
Augusta, NJ 07822
www.bantamclub.com

American Brahma Club
Sandy Kavanaugh, secretary/treasurer
216 Meadowbrook Rd.
Richmond, KY 40475

American Pastured Poultry Producers Association
www.apppa.org

American Poultry Association
Pat Horstman
PO Box 306
Burgettstown, PA 15021
724-729-3459
www.amerpoultryassn.com/APA_ShoppingMall3.htm

Araucana Club of America
www.auracana.net

Dominique Club of America
Bryan K. Oliver
948 West Bear Swamp Rd.
Walhalla, SC 29691
www.dominiqueclub.org
"Boosting America's oldest breed."

Nankin Club of America
www.nankinbantams.com
Promoting the rare, beautiful little Nankin bantam.

Plymouth Rock Fanciers Club of America
Robert Blosl, secretary/treasurer
14390 South Blvd.
Silverhill, AL 36576
www.crohio.com/rockclub

Polish Breeders Club
Jim Parker
3232 Schooler Rd.
Cridersville, OH 45806

Society for Preservation of Poultry Antiquities (SPPA)
$15 membership fee to Dr. Charles Everett
1057 Nick Watts Road
Lugoff, SC 29078
www.poultrybookstore.com
"Saving rare breeds from extinction."

Feeds and Nutrition

BovidRx Laboratories, Inc.
1-800-658-4016
www.bovidr.com
Nutri-Drench Poultry™.

Countryside Natural Products
1688 Jefferson Hwy.
Fishersville, VA 22939
www.countrysidenatural.com
Certified organic feeds.

The Fertrell Company
PO Box 265
Bainbridge, PA 17502
1-800-347-1566
www.fertrell.com
Natural and organic animal nutrition products.

Helfter Feeds, Inc.
866-35-3837
www.helfterfeeds.com
Certified organic feeds.

Modesto Milling
1-800-897-9740
www.modestomilling.com
100 percent organic feed manufacturer.

Natures Grown Organics
www.naturesgrownorganics.com
Organic feed.

The Work Schedule

When you take on the responsibility of caring for a living animal such as a chicken, certain tasks must be performed in a timely manner. There aren't a lot of tasks, and they're not difficult, but be prepared to work them into your schedule.

Chicks

On Arrival

- Have the brooder set up and tested (temperature 95°F) before the chicks arrive.

- Dip each chick's beak in the waterer as you remove it from the box.

- Observe their activity. If they huddle together, they're probably cold; if they're panting, they're too hot. Watch for any that don't act alert and active.

Daily

- Clean the feeder and waterer and be sure the chicks have a fresh supply of both at all times.

- Remove wet litter and add fresh.

- Observe chicks; watch for spraddle legs, pasty bottoms, and any signs of pecking on toes or emerging feathers.

Weekly

- Lower the brooder temperature by 5°F a week.

- Scrub and disinfect the waterer with a bleach solution (2 tablespoons household bleach to 1 gallon of warm water) and rinse thoroughly.

- Change litter as needed.

- When chicks are about 10 weeks old, or the brooder temperature is about equal to the outside temperature, the chicks can go into their outdoor coop.

- Switch from starter to grower rations according to the label of the feed you're using.

Pullets and Layers

- Continue to provide and monitor feed and water daily.

- For predator protection, close the chickens in their house every night at dusk, and open the house in the morning.

- Watch the birds regularly, not only with your eyes (mites, lice, pecking) but also with your ears (unusual breathing sounds, alarm calls) and your nose (any ammonia smell means it's past time to clean). Inspect premises for any signs of rodents or other pests and take appropriate action.

- Gather eggs at least once a day.

- Remove and compost accumulated manure and wet litter as necessary; clean and disinfect feeders and waterers as necessary, sometimes daily in hot weather when algae accumulates in water.

Index

CHECK OUT THESE BEST-SELLERS

More than 450 titles available at booksellers and online retailers everywhere!

978-1-59257-115-4

978-1-59257-900-6

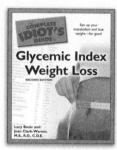

978-1-59257-855-9

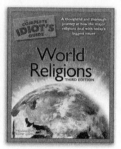

978-1-59257-222-9

978-1-59257-957-0

978-1-59257-785-9

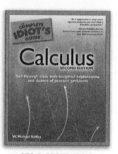

978-1-59257-471-1

978-1-59257-483-4

978-1-59257-883-2

978-1-59257-966-2

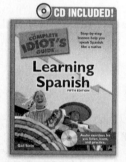

978-1-59257-908-2

978-1-59257-786-6

978-1-59257-954-9

978-1-59257-437-7

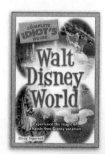

978-1-59257-888-7

ALPHA   idiotsguides.com